How to Swing in Musical Theatre

How to Swing in Musical Theatre shines a light on the most universal techniques used by cast members who, in response to absence, can perform multiple roles across an ensemble.

This entertaining guide can be used not only to build a step-by-step understanding of what swinging is and how it can be approached, but also as a constant point of reference throughout a career in musical theatre. Providing a suite of practical, technical advice on everything from quick and easy notation to compiling one's own personal swing 'bible', everything that an aspiring or experienced musical theatre performer will need is clearly arranged and thoughtfully explained. This book also teaches the SAFE Strategy, which is recognised as the most functional swing method and introduces the SAFE Principles of Swinging: Safety, Awareness, Function and Evolution. The principles are an original construct, devised to ward off stress and invite positive experience through reasoned behaviours.

Musical theatre performers at every level of the profession will find this an invaluable guide that elevates their craft no matter what their previous training, experience or success in the industry.

Jaye J. Elster traverses work as a director, choreographer and passionate guest lecturer for musical theatre institutes worldwide. As a professional actress, her West End credits include *Half a Sixpence*, *Matilda the Musical* and *Singin' in the Rain* – a production she continues to oversee internationally.

JAYE J. ELSTER

How to Swing in Musical Theatre
A Guide to Covering the Ensemble

Taylor & Francis Group

LONDON AND NEW YORK

Designed cover image: © Photo credit: Danny Kaan; Costume Design by Paloma Young for *& Juliet*, Shaftesbury Theatre; featuring Suki Wong, Zara Mackintosh, Collette Guitart, Cassandra Lee, Bessy Ewa, Sophie Usher, Rhian Duncan, Ebony Clarke and Rachel Moran.

First published 2024
by Routledge
4 Park Square, Milton Park, Abingdon, Oxon OX14 4RN

and by Routledge
605 Third Avenue, New York, NY 10158

Routledge is an imprint of the Taylor & Francis Group, an informa business

© 2024 Jaye J. Elster
© All illustrations by Dan Ioannou

The right of Jaye J. Elster to be identified as author of this work has been asserted in accordance with sections 77 and 78 of the Copyright, Designs and Patents Act 1988.

All rights reserved. No part of this book may be reprinted or reproduced or utilised in any form or by any electronic, mechanical, or other means, now known or hereafter invented, including photocopying and recording, or in any information storage or retrieval system, without permission in writing from the publishers.

Trademark notice: Product or corporate names may be trademarks or registered trademarks, and are used only for identification and explanation without intent to infringe.

British Library Cataloguing-in-Publication Data
A catalogue record for this book is available from the British Library

Library of Congress Cataloging-in-Publication Data
Names: Elster, Jaye, author.
Title: How to swing in musical theatre: a guide to covering the ensemble / Jaye Elster.
Description: [1.] | Abingdon, Oxon; New York: Routledge, 2023. | Includes index.
Identifiers: LCCN 2023003895 (print) | LCCN 2023003896 (ebook) | ISBN 9781032183909 (hardback) | ISBN 9781032183893 (paperback) | ISBN 9781003254300 (ebook)
Subjects: LCSH: Acting in musical theater.
Classification: LCC MT956 .E47 2023 (print) | LCC MT956 (ebook) | DDC 792.602/8—dc23
LC record available at https://lccn.loc.gov/2023003895
LC ebook record available at https://lccn.loc.gov/2023003896

ISBN: 9781032183909 (hbk)
ISBN: 9781032183893 (pbk)
ISBN: 9781003254300 (ebk)

DOI: 10.4324/9781003254300

Typeset in Joanna
by codeMantra

For my grandparents, Ron, Kathleen, Gordon and Celia,
The original lovers of sharing a good dance and
jolly sing song.
With love,
Jaye x

Contents

Foreword   xi
Acknowledgements   xii

Introduction   1

What is a swing? One   7
    Company structure   7
    Ensemble vs. swing   13
    What type of performer are you?   14

How to think like a swing Two   17
    The SAFE Principles   17

Strategies for every swing Three   25
    The One-Track-At-A-Time Strategy   25
    What is a swing bible?   29
    The SAFE Strategy   30
    Understanding ingredients and variables   31
    How will you swing?   32
    How to use this book   33
    Considerations   37

Success before you begin Four   39
    What's inside a swing's rucksack?   39
    A blueprint   43
    Final preparations   45

How to learn the ingredients Five   49
    Why the body stores the ingredients   49
    Choosing which ingredients to practice   50

All variables and no ingredients	51
Rehearsing ingredients in formation	52
Beware of the minimal cast change	53
Harmonies: ingredient or variable?	54
The SAFE Strategy for learning ingredients	56

How to record the variables Six 59

Long-life rehearsal notes	60
Minimum presentation checklist	64
Rehearsal room priority	66

Basics of notation Seven 69

How to record who tracks are	69
How to record where tracks are	72
Crosshairs	74
How to record where tracks travel	76
Arrows	77
Two types of traffic	78
Two types of arrow	79
Multiple tracks at a junction	80
After stage left	81
Multiple tracks at multiple junctions	82
How to record when	84
Scene work vs. production numbers	85
Shorthand for counts	86
Shorthand for duration	89

Speed of notation Eight 93

Common rehearsal room abbreviations	94
Speed charting	96
The tracks swings do not cover	98
Middle charting	101
Direction vs. traffic	102
Recording canon	105
Shorthand for lyrics	107
Consistency of shorthand	107

Information overload **Nine** 111
How to limit priorities 112
Video recording 113
Teamwork 118
Manage your expectations 120

Ready. Set. Swing bible. **Ten** 125
Tidying a swing bible 126
Ordering a swing bible 128
Optimising a swing bible 128
A choice of perspective 130
Minimum presentation checklist 2.0 131
Use of shorthand in a swing bible 134
Pencil & paper vs. computer software 137

Speed of extraction **Eleven** 141
Extracting position 141
Storyboards 143
Layers 145
Sidenotes 150
Quick Reference Grids (QRGs) 152
Which presentation method should I use? 152
Page layout 155
Cheat sheets 157
Track cards 160

In the performance space **Twelve** 163
In tech: swing priority 163
Studying the stage 165
Studying backstage 168
Entrances & exits 170
Shadowing tracks 171
Stamina of focus 174
Rehearsal room attachment disorder 175

Swing maps vs. cheat sheets **Thirteen** 179
The SAFE Strategy: in full 180
Cheat sheets: the advantages 182
Swing maps: the advantages 182

The minimum swing workload	184
How to stay in the fast lane	190

Specialist Swing Skills (S.S.S.) **Fourteen** 193

Partnering	193
Tracking props	195
Tracking set	196
Handling props & set	197
Split-Tracks	198
Swinging across gender	200
Recognising intention	201
Be accountable	202
The SAFER Principles	203
Remain calm	203
Swing self-care	205

How to look after a swing brain **Fifteen** 207

Know the myths	207
Manage blame	208
Remember your 'why'	208
A jack-of-all-trades but master of none	209
Always present, skillfully unseen	210
The performer bucket list	211
The swing sentence	211
Swings in the public eye	212

Outro 213

Glossary	217
Contributors	223
Index	225

Foreword

I was a swing on *Cats The Musical*. I covered nine tracks of which three were parts, and within my first six months on the show I had performed all nine of them. It was only my third professional show in the West End and to this day I describe it as one of the scariest and most challenging highlights of my career. Swinging taught me a discipline and gave me an understanding of how theatre works that no other role within the company could have. It was an unforgettable and invaluable learning curve.

Sometimes, it can feel like a thankless job or that you are being taken for granted as it's extremely hard, but I believe that the mentality towards swings is very much changing for the better – at last! Covid undoubtedly drew attention to the integral worth of swings as productions took extra precaution by hiring more. Without them, many more shows might have been forced to close.

When I cast swings, I look for astounding focus and the ability to pick up quickly, which enables a swing to morph into ensemble roles as soon as rehearsals begin. A swing is someone who thrives when rising to the extreme challenges that are set before them. They need to be hardworking, dedicated and positive-minded. Thankfully, whoever picks up this book is lucky to have the opportunity to learn from one of the best in the business.

For performers present and future, this book will give you the opportunity to learn the skills that will help you manage exactly how much work goes into swinging and ensure that you get the most out of the experience. I for one have complete respect and admiration for those that take on this vital role and can safely say that we couldn't do it without you. You are the cogs of a well-oiled machine that no matter which part fails, you replace it and keep the engine running perfectly!

Stephen Mear
Director and Choreographer

Acknowledgements

First, I would like to thank my family: my parents, Zena and Malcolm, my sister Laura and my brother Alex. I can be hellish when I put my mind to something and yet they continue to love and support me through every endeavour, at every turn. Thank you for letting me take advantage of your patience, entertaining the favours I ask of you from the more subtle 'what's the word I'm looking for?' to the blatant 'will you proofread this for me in your non-existent spare time?' But, I am most thankful for the magical way you always turn stressful moments into silly ones.

In 2010 I was given an opportunity, without which I would never have dreamed of publishing a book. The driving force behind that opportunity was director and choreographer Stephen Mear, who offered me my first professional swing contract. To Stephen, you set me on the path that has brought me untold joy, lifelong friends and unforgettable memories. Thank you for your continued support and for the inspiring foreword you have given to How to Swing in Musical Theatre.

Upon first pitching the idea to my former swing teammate and illustrator of this book, Dan Ioannou, he took me to the nearest literary shop in Covent Garden on the hunt for graphic inspiration. To Dan, thank you for your endless attention to detail, and for making me go back to the drawing board when I least wanted to. Fortunately, given your extraordinary skills at the drawing board, you proved to me every time that it was worth it in the end. The teaching power of this book is indebted to you, your talent and your ability to make an excellent cup of coffee over a Sunday working session.

I have spent the last decade wondering what How to Swing in Musical Theatre would look like, mainly because it has existed in my imagination in multiple capacities. Will it be interactive? Should it talk about my personal experience? Is my work as a dance captain relevant? In that time, there have been countless conversations with friends, family and colleagues which gave way to even more twists and turns in its conception. Whether knowingly or not, I would like to thank you all for helping me to realise the book in my head; I smile when I retrace so many parts of it back to an unassuming phone call or lunch date we had.

I would like to thank my teacher and friend Nikki Woollaston for her insistence that I re-visit life as a student to make sure the research needed to write the book would meet academic standards. During this time, I took a group of third year students to meet and interview the original swing company of *Hamilton* at the Victoria Palace Theatre, London who I would like to thank individually for sharing their honest swing experiences. They are, Jon Scott Clark, Lia Given, Barney Hudson, Phoebe Liberty, Alexzandra Sarmiento and Lindsey Tierney.

When theatre was forced to close at the beginning of the pandemic, I was lucky enough to test my swing method on a selection of students at various higher education institutes via video conferencing. I am extremely grateful to those institutes who opened their virtual doors to me: Millennium Performing Arts, The MTA, MADD College, Arts Educational Schools London, Italia Conti, London Studio Centre and MEPA Training. Some of my expert swing friends generously donated their time to meet the students I was working with. Thank you to Olly Christopher, Peter Houston and Olivia Sian Evans for the generosity you showed and for the positive message you help to spread about swinging in musical theatre.

To my brilliant and loyal agent, Mark Ward, thank you for your constant support, sending me regular texts dating back to 2013 to ask if book progress was being made. He connected me with casting director and swing advocate Jill Green, who I would like to thank for kindly providing a statement which endorsed the book for publication. Thank you also to Kristyn Coutts for inviting me to write an educational piece about swings on behalf of Spotlight UK and editor Christine Carè, for the help you provided in strengthening my book proposal.

I am forever grateful to my good friend Nick Butcher, who continues to donate his wonderful friendship and business acumen to me. He guided me into the capable hands of The Society of Authors and the brilliant Elizabeth Haylett Clark, who I would like to thank for helping me to both understand and navigate the legal stuff.

At Routledge, I would like to say thank you to Ben Piggott for picking my book proposal out of many during the 2020 lockdown before recommending it for publication and Steph Hines for being my thoroughly approachable and knowledgeable editorial assistant.

In 2017 I launched a survey and asked the world of social media to direct as many swings as possible, around the globe, to participate. I was overcome by the response and want to express my sincere thanks to anyone who helped spread awareness of the survey or took the time to share their experience with me. Without the data it collected, this book would not be able to speak to as many learning styles as it now does.

In 2022, I was awarded a grant from The Society of Authors and K Blundell Trust – specifically The Michael Meyer Award, in memory of Michael Meyer, who wrote about the theatre and translated the plays of Ibsen and Strindberg. I am grateful for the time they afforded me to make sure I was satisfied with every detail of the book ahead of final manuscript submission (like being able to appropriately thank those who helped me along the way). For any aspiring authors, I highly recommend looking up their support schemes to find out how they can help you too.

Finally, you will find I have used each situational example throughout the book to chronologically acknowledge my ex-swing teammates. I owe thanks to every one of you because I would not love swinging in musicals as much as I do, without the best memories I have of being one alongside you.

Introduction

On Tuesday 15 February 2011, watching the press night of *Shoes the Musical* in London's West End, I experienced one of the biggest performing thrills imaginable. No sooner than the lights came up on the interval, the associate choreographer of the show tapped me on the shoulder to let me know a performer had rolled her ankle and so for the rest of the performance I would perform in her place. I quickly gave up my seat in the stalls and made my way backstage to get ready for the second act. But I am not a professional theatre enthusiast who waits for injury to plague the West End, I am a professional performer employed to cover absence on a production, I am a swing though more accurately now, I had a successful career as one.

I had spent the previous month and a half on the side-lines of the *Shoes* rehearsal room, meticulously learning six different versions of the show as performed by six different cast members. It was my job to cover their absence if, for any reason, they were unable to perform over the course of the production run. In the decade that passed, I lost count of the number of times I stepped in mid-show like I did that night in 2011. My best chance of knowing when I would perform, and as who for that matter, was if a cast member had booked a holiday in advance. But make no mistake, live theatre is every bit as unpredictable as its reputation. Once the curtain rises, a swing should never expect to finish a show as they started it, be that watching from the auditorium, residing in their dressing room or performing on the stage itself.

Theatres around the world rely daily on their contingency system for absence which is made up of many different roles and responsibilities. You may have already heard of some of theatre's contingency chess pieces, such as understudies who are responsible for covering named or principal roles in a musical. Audiences will be made aware when they perform through updated billing on websites, in-house announcements, foyer notices and paper slips in show programmes. These announcements are the main reason the work of understudies is more widely known than that of their covering counterparts, swings, who step in unannounced to cover absence amid the choral parts that collectively make up the ensemble.

So, when a principal role or named role is absent, their understudy will cover and when an ensemble member is absent, a swing will cover. But it is not always as simple as exchanging one performer for another. For example, when an understudy performs, there is often a lengthier knock-on effect to the covering system. As the understudy steps up to play a principal role, a gap in the cast structure is left where they once were, commonly in the ensemble. Since ensemble parts are covered by swings, a swing will need to fill the resulting gap. Just like that, one absence draws two contingency roles into play: first, the understudy and second, the swing.

There are some even more complicated cast structures that see a slew of performers take on different roles from their usual to cover a single absence. This is made more likely when the principal role absent is of a specific casting requirement, for example in terms of age.

Lastly, when a production is tasked with covering multiple absences in the same performance, a gigantic juggling act of understudies and swings is set in motion. What is guaranteed is that every absence, whether of the principal or ensemble kind, results in a gap in the ensemble cast which is covered by a swing. Put it that way and you won't be surprised to know that at any given performance of a long-running production there is a strong, almost certain possibility that a swing is in play.

The difference between understudies and swings however, extends beyond the definition that one covers principal roles and the other covers the ensemble. I like to think of the term understudy as an additional responsibility assigned to any type of performer in a production. Whereas swings, like principal roles and ensemble members, *are* a type of performer. That is to say that principal roles, ensemble members, and swings can all take on understudy responsibilities or be referred to as 'understudies' informally.

In comparison to the swing experience, there is no denying that understudies have increased support. Most notably, an understudy benefits from a separate rehearsal process which will ensure they have time with any relevant technical elements and are given a dress rehearsal. The resident creative team will schedule and lead the understudy rehearsals, with many shows endeavouring to fully prepare their team of understudies by the time a show is said to be 'open'. By contrast, providing they show no visible signs of distress, swings face learning everything they need to know to cover absence as an entirely independent task-force.

When it comes to what constitutes as 'everything a swing needs to know', that workload is decidedly heftier than that of an understudy too.

In my experience of UK theatre practice, a performer on a musical might be an understudy for one or two roles, while a swing might expect to cover anywhere between three and eight ensemble roles.

The current Society of London Theatre (SOLT) Agreement for West End Theatre Artists demands that producers will provide adequate cover for potential absence but, there are no strict limitations on the number of understudy responsibilities a performer can assume or the number of ensemble roles a swing can be asked to cover.

It would be rare for an understudy to cover three or more named roles because the casting team would have growing concerns about the practicality of the covering system and mounting workload for the performer in mind. A soaring covering responsibility for swings however cannot be looked after in the same way. Whatever number of performers make up an ensemble cast, a swing will be asked, on some level, to cover. How do they remember it all?

As a young performer in amateur productions, I remember racing to the stage door to meet my family and to hear my grandmother ask with wonderment that very question, 'how do you remember it all?' It is true, performers have long since baffled non-performers by their ability to remember dialogue, choreography and lyrics, but swings surpass the average performer feat by a country mile.

Despite the longstanding need for musical theatre swings, the topic of how to swing remains somewhat unchartered territory. Truthfully, the vastness of the role and diverse learning styles of each swing has deterred anyone from trying to establish a formal method. So long as the skill of swinging appears impossible to explain, swings continue to suffer insufficient training and support. As a result, there exists a large pool of performers who believe they are neither capable of swinging nor 'the right fit' for the role, which is our current sad but honest reality.

Using the blueprint of a standard West End musical as an example, there might be six female ensemble tracks, six male ensemble tracks and a team of four swings. Excluding principal roles, swings make up 25% of the performer vacancies on that particular contract. In an already competitive industry, no performer should have to turn down a quarter of their career opportunities because of false beliefs about their ability to swing.

I started out as a swing. Since then, I have worked with some of the most formidable names in choreography and built relationships which undoubtedly gave way to my career as a director and choreographer today. But the onward career paths of previous swings are bountifully more varied than my steady climb up the creative ladder.

Even though swinging can serve as a brilliant career launchpad, that should not deter performers from traversing between both ensemble and swing contracts throughout their career. The industry is teeming professionals who choose not to limit themselves by being regarded as any one type of performer, myself included. I made my debut as ensemble in *Fame*, I went on to swing in *Shoes the Musical* before being given the choice between offstage swing and an ensemble role when *Singin' in the Rain* transferred to the West End.

As a swing, I remember show set-ups that were so dangerously thin on the ensemble ground that I would forgive myself for feeling like a superhero jumping from quick change to quick change, reappearing as multiple aliases. I had the most elaborate costume wardrobe in the dressing room, got paid more than my ensemble counterparts and never suffered from the monotony of playing the same eight shows in one week. Putting the careers and opportunities that can be born of swinging aside, I chose to be a swing simply because I had more fun being one.

In 2013, believing every performer deserves to be taught how to swing, I set about the previously unthinkable, conceiving a methodology for swinging. I collated everything I had learnt from my career as a swing, not omitting my mistakes, and cross referenced my experience with swings around the world. What I discovered is all here for you to read in *How to Swing in Musical Theatre*. It represents the closest thing in existence to a formal swing method and with it, I hope all performers are finally given the keys to the complete spectrum of performing careers.

If you are interested in a career as a swing, *How to Swing in Musical Theatre* will teach you step by step how to manage the impending workload and help you to develop a preliminary method that is tailored to both your learning style and the production you join.

If you're a performer who fears the swing role, *How to Swing in Musical Theatre* will make swinging accessible to you by offering the help, chronological advice, tips and techniques that were perhaps missing from your musical theatre training.

If you're a performer with swing experience or current swing, *How to Swing in Musical Theatre* will make for overdue assistance. You might seek problem specific advice or find ways to further refine your self-developed swing method for optimum efficiency and happiness.

If you're a performer who thinks they know confidently that they do not wish to swing, How to Swing in Musical Theatre will teach you how you can be of best support to the swings around you or more optimistically, empower you to give it a go.

And for the theatre enthusiasts among you, How to Swing in Musical Theatre will go some way to explaining exactly how swings remember it all.

1. WHAT IS A SWING?

What is a swing?

One

To be successful in any role, you must first understand how your role functions inside the company infrastructure. Think of it as a mechanical part inside a machine, to understand it you must know what it connects to and why. Successful swings understand how they connect to other roles inside a company and anticipate the ways they might interact.

COMPANY STRUCTURE

Figure 1.1 represents what is the most recognisable interpretation of how roles relate to each other on a standard musical. The top half of the structure makes up the primary creative team: producer, director, choreographer and musical supervisor.

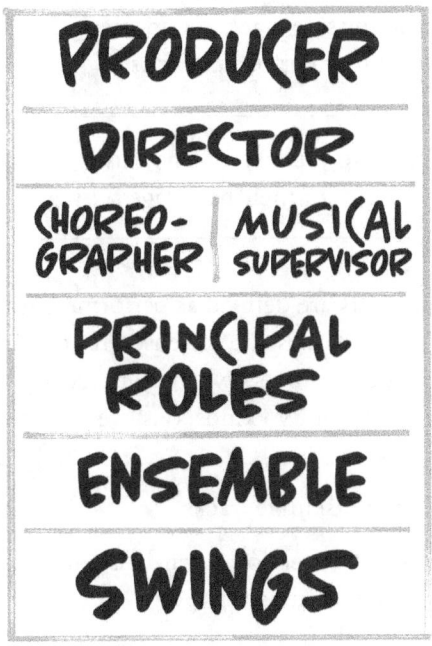

Figure 1.1 Company family tree A

DOI: 10.4324/9781003254300-2

The bottom half comprises of the cast: principal roles, ensemble and swings (please note, the term principal role hereafter encompasses supporting and featured roles).

Because swings are not guaranteed to perform nightly, they can easily be mistaken for a separate talent pool from what is deemed 'the cast'. In the name of respecting swings, and the role that they play in theatre, I should reiterate that they are very much a part of the cast and an integral one at that.

> CAST: The entire collection of performers that could potentially play in a production.

A more useful subdivision to identify would be the difference between onstage cast and offstage cast.

Despite the name, you cannot simply identify onstage cast just by looking at which performers are on stage during a performance. Some (or more) of the performers that you see might be offstage cast covering for absence.

When a member of the onstage cast is absent from a production, it falls to another cast member to step into the resulting gap, known professionally as 'the missing track'. Fundamentally, all productions are made up of a collection of performer tracks.

> TRACK: The complete journey of one onstage cast member in a performance, inclusive of their backstage activity.

Onstage cast members are defined as performers who possess a track in a production. Principal roles and the ensemble cast fall neatly into this category. Swings are cast members who cover absent ensemble tracks but interestingly, they can be of two kinds: onstage and offstage.

> SWING: A cover for ensemble tracks.
>
> ONSTAGE SWING: A cover for absent ensemble tracks who also possesses their own ensemble track.
>
> OFFSTAGE SWING: A cover for absent ensemble tracks who does not possess their own ensemble track.

Unlike principal roles or ensemble cast, the ensemble track of an onstage swing is created in such a way that if it were to be removed, the knock-on effect of absence to the production would be minimal. For this reason, their tracks stick to more central positioning and refrain from taking major responsibility in scene changes or having solo features. In other words, when an onstage swing is required to cover an ensemble absence, it is intended that they could relinquish their own ensemble track entirely in order to step into the missing ensemble track.

This, at least, is the theory behind the concept of onstage swings. From my experience, I have yet to know of an onstage swing track that is perfectly dispensable. When onstage swings cover ensemble absence, they will more than likely perform a hybrid track which combines the missing ensemble track with parts of their own that cannot be lost from the production.

As the name would suggest, offstage swings do not perform nightly. During a performance they are commonly found on standby in theatre dressing rooms or watching the show from the auditorium which is aptly known as conducting a show watch.

> SHOW WATCH: To observe a performance from the auditorium. Commonly, undertaken by cast to enhance professional performance and creatives to monitor show quality.

On occasions, offstage swings might know in advance that they are due to perform if, for example, they are covering annual leave or a long-term injury. Pending last-minute changes of circumstance, the earliest any swing, whether onstage or offstage, will have their track confirmed is on the day of performance by their company manager.

> COMPANY MANAGER: Central administrative role responsible for overseeing the day-to-day running of a theatrical production. Primary duties include handling payroll, scheduling, press, events, holidays, health and safety, ticket requests, training and bridging communications across all departments.

Giving swings fair notice about which tracks they will cover before a performance is reliant on the compliance of the full cast to report individual absence, to the company manager, prior to an agreed cut-off time. Performers should note that this time will differ on matinee performance days. Once it is confirmed which onstage tracks are absent, a basic show set-up is agreed upon by an in-house team and circulated by the company manager to all necessary departments.

> SHOW SET-UP: Daily summary of absence and break down of cast covering.

Swings will be given the daily show set-up by phone call, text or email and if necessary, a more detailed version will be issued that could include choreographic adjustments, additional quick changes and reallocated lines (whether spoken or sung).

The show set-ups are displayed on a company notice board, commonly located close to the stage door entrance of a theatre. On arrival before a performance, it is the job of all departments to check the company notice board for announcements. All cast members should check the notice board for any last-minute changes to the planned show set-up.

So, as their names would suggest, onstage swings are categorised as onstage cast, alongside principal roles and ensemble performers, and offstage swings make up some of the offstage cast. Offstage swings might also be joined by performers known as alternates and standbys who predominantly identify as offstage cast.

> ALTERNATE: A performer who regularly plays a principal role but has less scheduled performances per week than the performer cast in the role concerned. They are often cast when a role is physically or vocally demanding.
>
> STANDBY: An offstage performer who is available to play a principal role under unscheduled circumstances such as in an emergency. They are cast for roles that are physically or vocally demanding or have time consuming makeup, wig or wardrobe requirements.

How many swings a production requires and of what kind will depend on several factors including cast size, contract length and whether the production is to take up residency or tour multiple venues. Swing teams therefore come in all varieties: those made up exclusively of either onstage or offstage swings and those that combine the use of both.

In Figure 1.1 (see page 7), you will notice that 'understudies' are not represented. When a performer is heard being referred to as 'an understudy', it is a shortened way of saying that they have an understudy responsibility. Understudy is therefore not a job title and does not appear on diagrams describing company structure.

> UNDERSTUDY: A responsibility given to a member of cast to cover a principal or supporting role in case of absence.

Commonly it is misunderstood that understudy allocation is limited to ensemble cast members. As a responsibility and not a job title, both principal roles and swings can too be understudies. The kind of principal role capable of taking on an understudy responsibility however is of the supporting or featured kind. You would not, for example, find the actor playing Fagin understudying the role of Bill Sykes too often.

The question of how all of these different cast members – principal roles, ensemble and swings – relate to each other in practice requires a different, potentially less recognisable, diagram to describe company structure.

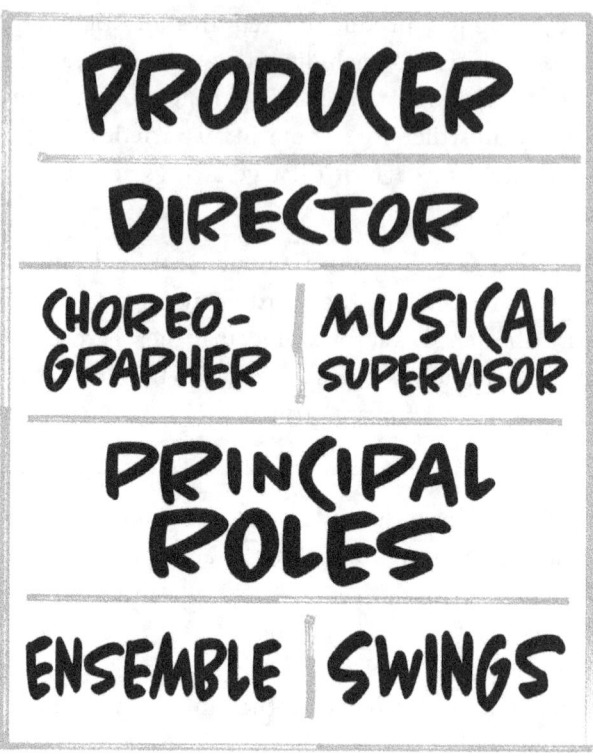

Figure 1.2 Company family tree B

If we interpret Figures 1.1 and 1.2 as family trees A and B respectively, family tree A depicts swings as descendants of the ensemble whereas B depicts swings and ensemble as siblings. While B is a truer reflection of company structure, many would accidentally describe family tree A before B.

Given that the definition of a swing is a cover for ensemble, it is easy to fathom how swings might be mistakenly ranked lower than ensemble performers. Sadly, this honest mistake has played a part in some considerable damage to the reputation of swings in time gone by. You see, so long as family tree A is more widely known to depict company structure, a long-standing misconception that swings are the hierarchical lesser of the ensemble prevails. It is a myth that continues to harm swing self-esteem and block entire career pathways.

Family tree A shouldn't be disregarded entirely, it can be useful to help describe how different roles contribute creatively to a production. Shows are created on the ensemble cast by embracing their unique skillset. As such it is fair to say that an ensemble would carry more creative influence than a covering team of offstage swings. Offstage swings who are appointed dance captain however present an exception to this generalisation.

DANCE CAPTAIN: A responsibility given to a member of cast to maintain the choreographic quality of a production. Duties include leading daily warm-up, facilitating understudy rehearsals and informing show set-ups.

Like an understudy, dance captain is a responsibility that can be assigned to any cast member. Given the nature of the role however, it almost always falls to an ensemble member or swing. Of the two, the latter is perhaps the more conventional choice. When an offstage swing is appointed dance captain, their close working relationship with the choreographer challenges the idea that all offstage swings bear less creative influence on a production than the ensemble.

ENSEMBLE VS. SWING

For the happiest and most effective musical companies, it is important for all who work within it to understand that the ensemble relate to swings as equals. We can initiate this shift through the simple practice of teaching it.

The very definitions of onstage swings and ensemble performers support equality between the two because, providing there are no cast absences, they both have the same job – to perform their ensemble track.

Like siblings, it would be difficult to compare the value of ensemble performers and swings, but it is easier to comment on their behavioural differences.

An ensemble member prioritises the quality of their individual performance, whereas a swing prioritises the mechanics of a production. Of course, a swing is not an all-singing, all-dancing shell of a performer, they surely 'perform', but when the magic of live theatre goes rogue, a swing's priority automatically falls to the show's function above the quality of their own performance.

Most performers pursue a career in musical theatre with plentiful ensemble training and minimal swing training. Behaviourally as performers, they are therefore more intrinsically wired for the ensemble role. Before these performers attempt to swing, they should anticipate how they might need to think differently to perform optimally as one.

> It is commonly thought that once you have swung, you won't look at theatre the same way again. The angle from which swings watch a show being created leads to a greater appreciation for the artful way all departments work together to arrive at opening night. It is what makes for a natural career progression from swing into more creative roles in the future.

WHAT TYPE OF PERFORMER ARE YOU?

The course content of professional theatre training institutes promotes the development of ensemble mindsets by largely assessing students according to the standard of their craft as individuals and as part of an onstage cast, which is to grade their ensemble skillset. Unfortunately, this educational bias can deny students the opportunity to find out which role they might enjoy more: ensemble or swing. To make matters worse, many performers graduate feeling ill-equipped to swing and prematurely decide to avoid the job opportunity altogether.

The number of swings to ensemble headcount in the industry is not as low as you might think, they account for a sizeable percentage of performer job vacancies. Add to this that many first jobs lead to the next and it is scary how many career pathways may have failed to launch because formal training has made it so easy for graduates to say 'no' to swinging.

If you have trained, or are currently training, to be a musical theatre professional, acknowledging the educational bias can protect you from limiting your career options. I believe everyone has a separate swing mindset (or ability to serve show function); they might just need a little extra guidance from *How to Swing in Musical Theatre* to unlock its full potential.

Once in possession of both ensemble and swing mindsets, you will unlock the opportunity to find out which role you like better through experience rather than assumption. Will you prefer performing in the ensemble, swinging or maybe even a bit of both?

At the end of this chapter, you should be able to:

❏ Confidently define Alternate, Cast, Company Manager, Dance Captain, Onstage Swing, Offstage Swing, Show Watch, Show Set-up, Standby, Swing and Track.
❏ Draw an honest family tree to describe company structure on a musical.
❏ Understand swings and ensemble to be of equal hierarchical value.
❏ Differentiate between the working approach of swings and ensemble performers.
❏ Comment on the quality of your own swing training.

2. HOW TO THINK LIKE A SWING

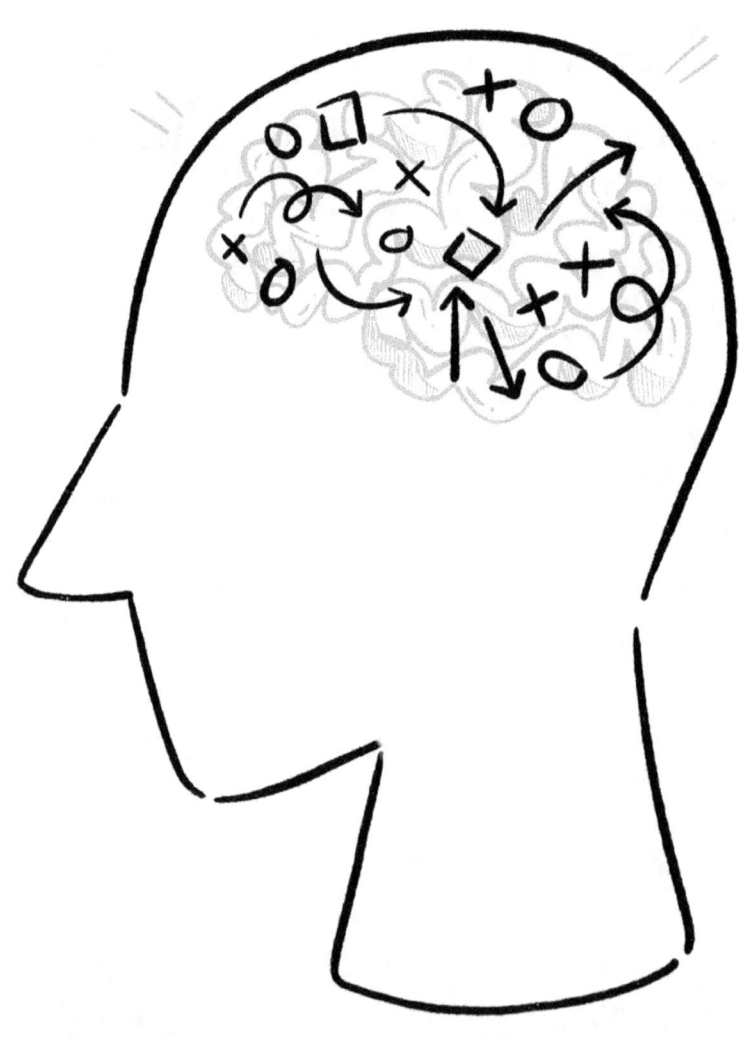

How to think like a swing

Two

In the previous chapter, we learnt that the mindset of a swing has a different focus from that of an ensemble member. To recap, an ensemble member prioritises the quality of their individual performance whereas a swing prioritises show function. To swing well then, a different mindset needs to be awakened, known more affectionately to most performers as 'the swing brain'. This might sound about as easy as having a brain transplant but before you book your consultation, we can achieve the same result less invasively by starting with the establishment of a new behavioural code of conduct.

A new behavioural what? Cast your mind back to spending the first lesson of each school year designing a new set of classroom rules. They would almost always include 'raise your hand to speak' and 'treat others as you would like to be treated'. By sticking to them, we stuck to a new behavioural code of conduct, and it enabled us to think and behave in a way that promoted our own success as well as the success of others. We can set some similar ground rules to make up a swing code of conduct which will help us to think differently from an ensemble performer and guide our behaviour as a swing.

THE SAFE PRINCIPLES

The following four principles provide a good template for swings to use as ground rules:

1. I will act in the name of safety first.
2. It is my job to be aware of what the entire stage is doing at any one given time.
3. My primary responsibility is to facilitate the function of the production.
4. I understand that a production is constantly shifting, evolving and changing.

Swings, no matter how experienced, will always encounter scenarios which cause them to feel uncertain, anxious, under pressure or any combination of the three. The four guiding principles above exist to act as a swing's best friend; swings can lean on them to help steer them out of trouble and in the direction of pro-activity.

S-Principle: safety

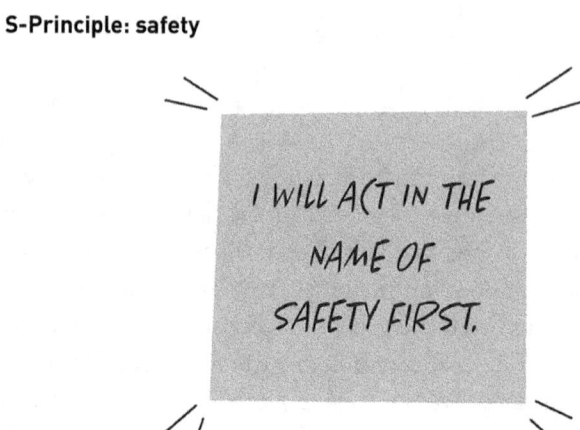

Figure 2.1 Quoted S-Principle

Working in a position which requires you to put the needs of others or something else above your own will inevitably lead to a slower reflex in terms of personal safety. Strange as it may sound, swings often find themselves caught in a dilemma between protecting their personal safety and serving show function.

There is no scenario that should ever cause a swing to risk the safety of themselves or others. It is the primary reason the Safety Principle, or S-Principle, sits proudly at the top of our guiding principles.

If a swing feels they are in danger or that they might be putting someone else at risk, they should report their concern to a member of the resident creative team, dance captain or company manager, at their earliest opportunity.

> RESIDENT CREATIVE TEAM: In-house directors, musical directors and choreographers that attend the day-to-day running of the show to maintain show quality on behalf of the creative team: directors, musical supervisors and choreographers.

A-Principle: awareness

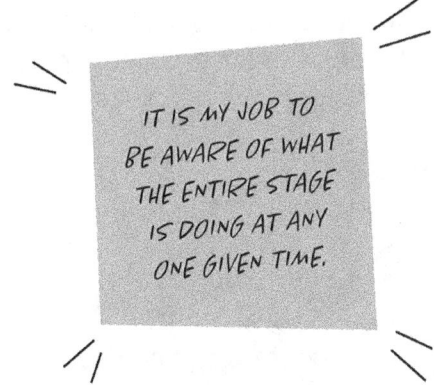

Figure 2.2 Quoted A-Principle

In the context of driving a car, reduced awareness compromises the safety of the driver, their passengers and their surroundings. So, in the first instance, the Awareness Principle, or A-Principle, acts as a support for satisfying the S-Principle; when we are aware, we are safe. Being aware as a swing however, carries far more advantages than the one of protecting safety:

Increased reaction speed
When the unpredictability of live theatre strikes, swings often act as first-responders to the scene. This might mean switching ensemble tracks, delivering a vocal line or striking an accidentally abandoned prop. To spot this unexpected need, swings must always maintain an awareness of the bigger picture in play.

Reduced workload
Familiarity with the bigger picture is a big assist for swings trying to process a lot of information in a finite amount of time. As opposed to remembering the individual positions of multiple ensemble tracks, many swings find it easier to instead recall the collective shape made by the position of all tracks, hereafter 'the formation' – a filled-in triangle or set of columns for instance.

Reasoned instincts

Knowledge of the overall formation is as much a learning assist as it is an informant. For example, when a swing doubts where to be on stage, an understanding of why the formation looks incomplete has the power to inform where they should be by process of elimination.

F-Principle: function

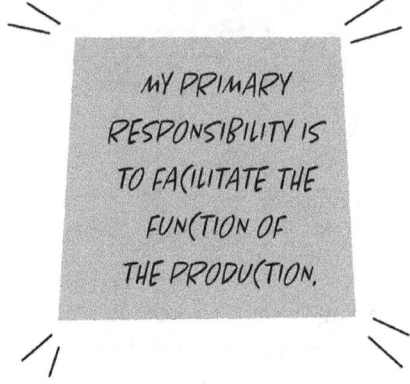

Figure 2.3 Quoted F-Principle

Swing pride hinges on an ability to serve show function, swings can practice this daily by continuously asking the question 'what can I do to help?' The answer highlights where to focus their attention, but occasionally it requires a swing to perform with some degree of inaccuracy.

> Imagine Track A leaves the main rehearsal room for a private dialect call and so a gap in the ensemble opens up. It would serve rehearsal function for Swing B to step in but, Swing B doubts how well they know Track A. In this situation, Swing B should ask themselves 'what can I do to help?' Much of the time the answer will sound like 'step in and do what you can, albeit badly'. Try not to let this scare you, it is surprising how much can be gained as a swing from getting stuck in, even when you feel out of your depth.

In rehearsal, when a swing steps in and struggles to forgive themselves for mistakes made, it is likely that they have not yet made the shift from an ensemble mindset (that of first satisfying personal performance standards) to a swing mindset (that of first serving show function).

Performers should not underestimate how difficult it is to switch off inherent perfectionism. Fortunately, remembering the F-Principle plays a crucial part in helping them to separate what is or is not worth worrying about. Be kind to yourself and accept that it may take some time to trust that a perfect job done by a swing lies in simply helping the show tell its story from curtain up to curtain down without interruption.

E-Principle: evolution

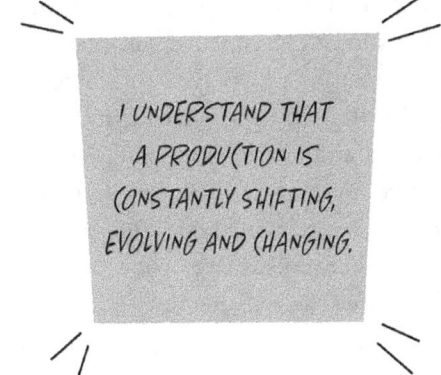

Figure 2.4 Quoted E-Principle

A production that requires swings will generally rehearse for a lesser number of weeks than the full length of the production run. Typically, a new West End musical might rehearse for four to twelve weeks before initiating a twelve-month run. It would be lovely to think that every decision made during the rehearsal period will prove appropriate for total contract length but alas, naïve. Productions inevitably mature beyond the rehearsal process and as onstage cast discover better choices through practice, swings are required to stay up-to-date with every shift. For example, a track might find more practical geography or a more consistent grip for a dance lift.

> Over time, swings that respect the A-Principle are better equipped to respect the E-Principle too. With their knowledge of the overall formation, they continually position themselves appropriately no matter whether the ensemble performers gradually drift by inches or metres from what was originally staged.

Swings invest an incredible amount of time and energy into learning and processing all that goes into creating a production. As a result, they can become extremely protective over every ounce of original detail they absorb. This is a wonderful quality to have as a swing but be warned, it can also cause resistant behaviour.

When a production matures or evolves, the resident creative team will make decisions to ensure a continued quality of show. On occasions, this will mean that re-instruction is given (in the form of 'notes', likely verbal) which could differ from original staging. In nature, notes will be of both the practical and artistic kind and may relate to individuals as well as the collective. The most well performing companies trust their resident creative teams to note in the best interests of the show and avoid interpreting notes, whether individual or collective, to bear reflection on their personal performance. So, where change causes no harm, it makes sense for onstage cast members to simply accept notes, no questions asked. If the phrase 'Just take the note' were to be sold on a t-shirt, it would make for a popular stocking filler in musical theatre circles.

For swings however, the smallest of changes can create a fair bit of additional work. Rather than dread change, the E-Principle reminds swings to expect and embrace it because their commitment to show quality matters more than the elevated workload change could cause.

Luckily, a nifty acronym can be used to remember these four guiding principles which when grouped together become the SAFE Principles of Swinging:

S is for Safety
A is for Awareness
F is for Function
E is for Evolution

To answer the question 'how do I rewire myself to think like a swing?', I simply encourage performers to let the SAFE Principles inform the decisions their swing brain makes. Looking ahead, we will continue to be reminded of these principles as we use them to guide our behaviour along every step of the production process.

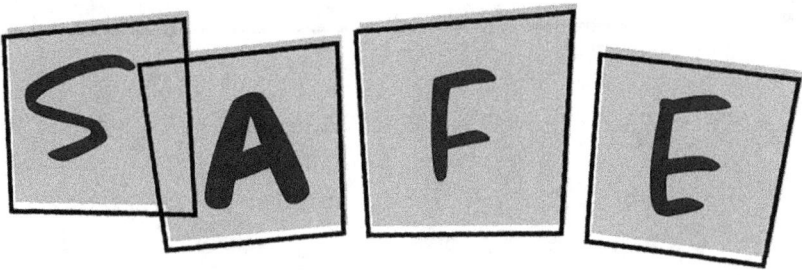

Figure 2.5 The SAFE Principles

At the end of this chapter, you should be able to:

❏ Recall the SAFE Principles of Swinging.
❏ Give practical reason for the individual importance of each SAFE Principle.
❏ Awaken your swing brain using the good steer of the SAFE Principles.

3. STRATEGIES FOR EVERY SWING

Strategies for every swing
Three

To best prepare for absence, a production may decide to offer swings a system of first and second cover allocation. This means that one swing will be first in line to cover a selection of ensemble tracks and second or even third in line to cover the remaining.

Though productions are not bound to use such a system, swings are encouraged to seek their allocation at the earliest opportunity from a dance captain. Knowing which tracks they are first in line to cover could inform their priority for learning and bring needed structure to their process.

Problematically, the level of comfort swings can yield from allocation only lasts so long. In fact, just one absence can overthrow the system. For example, when the first responsibility to cover eight ensemble tracks is shared equally between two swings, each swing prioritises four ensemble tracks. As soon as one swing is lost to an absence, the remaining swing becomes first cover for all seven of the remaining ensemble tracks. There is no way to predict the order in which illness or injury will strike and so do not dismiss the likelihood that, in a flash, you could be made first cover for all ensemble tracks.

Whether a system of swing allocation is used or not, a swing therefore needs to strategise for learning it all as quickly as possible.

THE ONE-TRACK-AT-A-TIME STRATEGY

As people, when we have a lot to achieve, we like to take things step-by-step where step one entails making a to-do list. For a swing with eight ensemble covers, tvhat might look a bit like this:

1. Learn track 1
2. Learn track 2
3. Learn track 3
4. Learn track 4
5. Learn track 5
6. Learn track 6

7. Learn track 7
8. Learn track 8

To learn what each cast member (i.e., track) does one by one shall hereafter be known as swinging 'One-Track-At-A-Time' (OTAAT swinging).

One of the key advantages of OTAAT swinging, is the ability it has to measure the working progress of a swing. In everyday life, we often take the progress bars around us for granted, not to mention the peace of mind they bring:

- Computer screens tell us how much of a program has been installed.
- Live departure boards count down the arrival of the next bus.
- Mobile phones track the progress of takeaway deliveries.

A swing using the OTAAT Strategy measures their progress by monitoring how many tracks they have learnt versus how many tracks they have yet to learn.

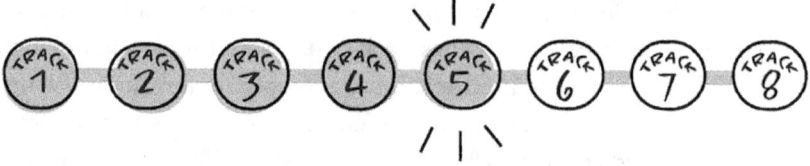

Figure 3.1 One-Track-At-A-Time progress bar

It is a very neat and tidy construct but, imagine you have journeyed along the OTAAT progress bar up as far as learning Track 5 (demonstrated by Figure 3.1). Now suppose that Track 8 calls off sick, despite your knowledge of five tracks, you would have good reason to panic. So, while the intent to learn all eight tracks was well-meaning, the OTAAT method leaves swings just as vulnerable as they would be if they solely prioritised learning their first covers ahead of any 'seconds' or 'thirds'.

There are other, more nuanced ways that the OTAAT method can limit the effectiveness of the swing using it.

Firstly, once the computer program loads, a bus arrives, or swing has learnt their total ensemble tracks, the progress bar could be viewed as complete. But is a complete OTAAT progress bar really the definition of job completion for swings? The reality for effective swings is that the job is never complete because productions, and more specifically tracks, never stop evolving.

Figure 3.2 E-Principle

Unfortunately, a complete progress bar for any swing is rather like a pot of gold at the end of a rainbow; it is always going to be just out of reach. To honour the E-Principle, they must accept that it will only ever reach 99% completion, while the remaining 1% remains open to and accepting of change.

Secondly, when swings learn one track at a time, their focus narrows to the immediate surroundings of one track, often neglecting the relationship the track concerned has with other tracks. It is as though they assume a sort of tunnel vision.

Figure 3.3 Tunnel vision

Given that having tunnel vision is the literal opposite of appreciating the bigger picture, OTAAT swings miss out on the advantages associated with maximal awareness, which were listed in Chapter 2 as:

- Safer decision making
- Increased reaction speed
- Reduced workload
- Reasoned instincts

Remember also, the covering system is not always as simple as exchanging one performer for another. Sometimes there are more ensemble tracks absent than there are swings to cover, which can require swings to combine ensemble tracks into hybrid tracks in a cut-show.

> CUT-SHOW: Term given to a reduced version of a production that has been reconfigured to meet the demands of extreme absence or technical hindrance.
>
> SPLIT-TRACK: A hybrid ensemble track performed by swings when required to cover more than one ensemble track in a single performance.

Albethey temporary, when a swing performs a hybrid track, professionally known as a 'split-track', they must prepare for the new ways they may encounter set and people. Imagine Track A and Track B are absent and only Swing C is available to cover. From show start to finish, decisions must be made about which track Swing C will cover. To preserve the prettiest picture on stage, it is decided that Swing C must cover Track A in one formation and Track B in a second. How Swing C transitions between the two formations will not be a routine journey and the potential for collision must be anticipated in advance.

OTAAT swings are very good at performing carbon copies of ensemble tracks but when needed to deviate from the norm, tunnel vision limits their ability to anticipate unusual journeys or positioning and their usefulness plummets.

When an OTAAT swing cannot be trusted to split-track, other swings, and even non-swings, may have to take on additional responsibility to make up for inflexibility within the swing team.

So, despite the advantages the OTAAT method has to offer in terms of:

a) Knowing how much more is yet to be learnt.
b) Dictating a natural order to learn information.

An OTAAT swing gambles with the order of absence and could dissatisfy:

1. The E- Principle if they wrongly assess their job to be complete.
2. The A-Principle if they assume tunnel vision.
3. The S-Principle if they attempt a split-track without due consideration for potential collision.
4. The F-Principle if they cannot be trusted to split-track.

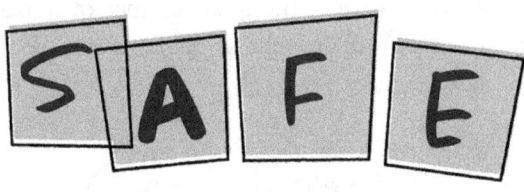

Figure 3.4 The SAFE Principles

That's all four of the SAFE Principles! There must be another way.

WHAT IS A SWING BIBLE?

Since insufficient awareness of the bigger picture is the catalyst for many an OTAAT swing problem, perhaps it makes more sense to replace learning one track at a time with learning one picture at a time. Imagine a production broken down into a flipbook of bird's eye sketches of the stage and you will start to picture something that looks remarkably like a swing bible.

> SWING BIBLE: The collective term given to documentation used by swings to assist the retention of information that cannot be recalled from memory.

Put simply, swing bibles serve to store the information that swings do not trust themselves to remember. Their content however is not limited to sketches alone but may also incorporate prose notes, photographs, voice recordings and videos.

While no two swing bibles will look the same, making one is without doubt the most universal thing swings do to learn multiple ensemble tracks in a musical. Frustratingly though, many swings know they want to make a swing bible but have no idea where to start...

THE SAFE STRATEGY

Created from research into the working methods of over 100 swings from around the world, the SAFE Strategy is an alternative swing method which, in its conception, sought to be the most universal and effective swing method. If indeed swing bibles are a universal tool among swings, let us hope that the SAFE Strategy might teach us how to make one.

First, it offers a new way of measuring a swing's progress. Instead of dividing their workload into the total number of tracks to learn, it categorises two areas for learning: the ingredients and the variables.

Figure 3.5 The SAFE Strategy: The workload of a swing

INGREDIENTS: Information, recalled from memory, pertaining to *what* tracks do; *what* steps they dance and *what* words they say.

VARIABLES: Recorded instructions that can change and affect the ingredients, differentiating one track from another. Variables predominantly inform the answers to *where*, *when* and *how* tracks do *what*.

Swings using the SAFE Strategy to learn multiple ensemble tracks will go about learning the ingredients and variables simultaneously. As a result, they learn a little bit of each track every step of the way. A progress bar for swings using the SAFE Strategy (hereafter 'SAFE swings') looks like this:

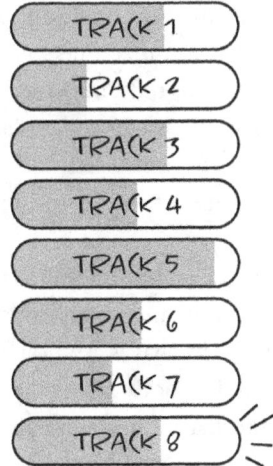

Figure 3.6 The SAFE Strategy progress bar

Imagine the SAFE swing whose progress bar looks like Figure 3.6. While it could feel uneasy not to know any one track in its entirety, if Track 8 were to call off sick, they would have every reason to feel somewhat smug that their progress bar does not look like Figure 3.1 (see page 26) which belongs to an OTAAT swing.

UNDERSTANDING INGREDIENTS AND VARIABLES

To help us better understand the difference between ingredients and variables we can break down tracks into function machines.

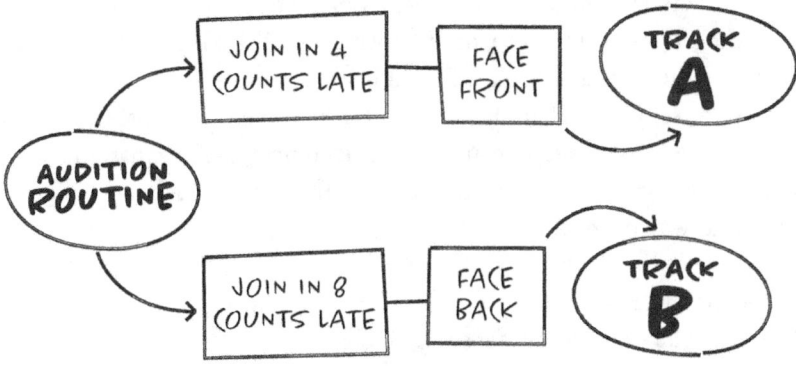

Figure 3.7 Track function machine

Here, each track dances the same choreography (or has the same ingredients) known as the "audition routine". When different instructions (or variables) are applied to the audition routine, such as those about timing and direction, the function machine spits out a different track.

For a closer analogy to ingredients and variables in everyday life, picture a raw egg. Treat the egg as an *ingredient* and leave it in boiling water for a *variable* amount of time. The resultant soft- and hard-boiled eggs can be likened to the production of Tracks A and B in Figure 3.7.

To name but a few other variables, tracks perform in different places on the stage, travel opposite ways and reverse choreography to lead with the right or left side of the body. That is a whole lot of variables to learn, so swings write them down. The body stores the ingredients (*what* tracks do), while paper – or an alternative electronic medium – remembers the variables (*where*, *when* and *how* they perform *what*).

To learn the ingredients in rehearsal, SAFE swings practice a template version upon which all tracks can be based and will hereafter be known as a 'template track'.

> TEMPLATE TRACK: Conceived ensemble track used by swings to embody a standard combination of ingredients against which all ensemble tracks can be closely compared.

In an ideal rehearsal scenario, a swing's template track consists of a 'one-size-fits-all' version of the ingredients so that they can step into any track, at any time, with reasonable accuracy.

SAFE swings keep on top of what all other tracks do by asking 'How does each track differ from my template track?' Each individual difference is defined as a variable and will be recorded.

In time, notes pertaining to the variables will be transferred to a swing bible for safe keeping and future reference. Just like that, the SAFE Strategy defines what to include in a swing bible and hence offers a structural way of making one:

1. Record all variables.
2. Arrange all variables into a swing bible.

HOW WILL YOU SWING?

To settle any lingering uncertainty you have over choosing to swing using the OTAAT Strategy or the SAFE Strategy, let us compare both methods in terms of workload.

OTAAT swings commit their focus to one track until that track is learnt in its entirety. Problematically though, there is no way of knowing if the track they chose to learn first is the most similar or dissimilar to other ensemble tracks. Forget gambling with ensemble absence, this means how much progress an OTAAT swing makes by learning their first track is luck of the draw.

Conversely, the first track a SAFE swing learns is their template track, which is made intentionally similar to all tracks so that a swing can step in at short notice during rehearsal. As they learn their template track then, they are guaranteed to be making the most significant dent possible in their workload as soon as they possibly can.

So, the choice is yours. Would you rather be an OTAAT swing and gamble with an already intimidating workload or guarantee maximum productivity by opting for the SAFE Strategy?

HOW TO USE THIS BOOK

It must come as no surprise that I am a cheerleader for using the SAFE Strategy to swing. Beyond simply recording the variables though, what are the intermediate steps swings take to become the keeper of a fully functional swing bible? And what are the intermediate steps swings take to claim confidently that they have learnt the ingredients?

Chapter by chapter, we are about to fill in the gaps, adding steps to our existing picture of the SAFE Strategy (see Figure 3.5, page 30) until we have built a flowchart which you are able to use as your step-by-step guide to:

1. Learning the ingredients.
2. Recording variables in a practical swing bible.
3. Swinging in musical theatre.

For any strategy to work for you, it needs to not only be tailored to who you are and how you learn but also the circumstances under which you are joining a company. Mostly, this book assumes that:

a) You are joining an original (that's never-before-performed) production as a swing.
b) You have no prior swing experience.

If either factor applies to you, you are advised to read this book cover to cover. On the other hand, let us suppose how this book can help a swing whose circumstances do not fit that mould.

Experienced swings

I invite swings with existing experience to discover in great depth how other swings around the world have been and are doing the same job.

Until now, your swing method will have been completely formulated through your own guesswork, creativity and lessons learnt through experience. This book provides an opportunity for you to collaborate with other swing minds to further refine your process. Your reward will be improved performance and a happier state of swinging. I predict your best eureka moments will happen between Chapter 5 – *How to record the variables* – and Chapter 11 – *Speed of Extraction*. Not forgetting, there will be some brilliant pearls of wisdom you can absorb from Chapters 14 and 15 too.

Being an onstage swing

One advantage of being an onstage swing is that your template track will be dictated to you in the form of your own ensemble track. Your job as an onstage swing will be to record the ways that all other ensemble tracks differ from your own and learn any additional ingredients (those you do not perform regularly in your own track) as necessary.

Unfortunately, the latter tasks are not to be underestimated. Onstage swings cannot be in constant possession of a notebook (though I would always give it your best shot). They cannot freely abandon one rehearsal room to go and spend some time in another. They might not be available to learn additional ingredients under the expectation of a choreographer who needs them to master their own. These are just some of the niches, but nonetheless common obstacles onstage swings face in rehearsal. Some of the tactics described in Chapter 9 – *Information Overload* – will greatly assist you in this respect.

To fulfil the role responsibilities of an onstage swing, they must often avoid volunteering for additional features during the creative process. Imagine rehearsing and caring for an ensemble track which, with the greatest respect to your talent, seeks to be dispensable. It can feel discouraging at times which is not helped by the pressure of learning multiple other ensemble tracks, all the while not feeling fully confident of your own. The onstage swing job tests the mind in ways that the offstage swing can only count themselves lucky. Chapter 15 – *How to look after a swing brain* – has some invaluable advice to share with you.

However frustrating passing up stage time can be as an onstage swing, when you are needed to cover an absent ensemble track, you will only be grateful for the ease with which you can at times abandon your own track to therefore perform a bit of both.

That said, there are plenty of upsides to being an onstage swing that can make it more enjoyable than being an offstage one. For example, thanks to the familiarity of performing nightly, onstage swings will be better prepared for what a costume or wig feels like to dance in, how bright the lights are on stage and what happens backstage. They are also more likely to take part in media events that require full ensemble participation.

Rehearsing a cast change or revival

Cast changes and revivals present a different rehearsal process for swings because the show already exists and hence the answer to the question 'what do I need to learn?' will be a lot more factual:

Learn these words. Sing these harmonies. Dance these steps. Wear these costumes. Be careful of that set piece. Put this chair here.

Providing the performance venue does not change in the handover between casts, you will be able to start making your swing bible from the outset of rehearsals without fear of information changing day-to-day (as it would do on a show in creation). For more advice on how you can optimise the information you put in your swing bible, see Chapter 7 – *Basics of Notation* – and Chapter 10 – *Ready, Set, Swing bible* – though I recommend stopping by the chapters in between.

Some productions might be so established that, as opposed to making your own swing bible, you receive a ready-made one. If this is your given scenario, please do not ignore or underestimate the following:

1. Swing bibles are unique.
    A single swing bible cannot be compatible with every swing that needs to use it. If that were true, I would have no rationale to write this book. Of course, a swing bible made by another is an extremely useful tool but to swing from it alone would inhibit your full swing potential. To

be the most effective swing you can be, you must tailor your swing bible in such a way that you can work quickly and accurately from it.

2. Learning by studying.

When students revise for an exam, they might make flash cards, invent acronyms or write things down from memory on repeat. It is not luck that they start to remember the information they are revising but a direct result of the study time they put in.

Swinging can be a high-pressure and time-sensitive job. The swing who accepts a ready-made swing bible misses out on the chance to absorb information by spending time studying it. As a result, they are more likely to swing slowly and permanently attached to the swing bible they did not make.

You can create study time with a ready-made swing bible by customising it with the ideas explored in Chapter 10 – *Ready. Set. Swing bible.* and Chapter 11 – *Speed of Extraction*.

Joining a company mid-contract

You may be joining a company mid-production run as an additional or replacement swing. If so, check out the advice given above to swings rehearsing for a cast change – you have a lot in common with them. Since the show pre-exists, you can make the same head start on the creation of your swing bible but take caution if you are provided with a ready-made one.

Figure 3.8 A-Principle

The distinctive challenge facing a swing in this scenario is that they are likely to rehearse in isolation or with a limited number of fellow joining cast members. Developing an appreciation for the bigger picture will therefore be made trickier with only a fraction of the full ensemble represented in the rehearsal room.

There is some good advice about how to combat a rehearsal room like this in Chapter 5 – *How to Learn the Ingredients*.

CONSIDERATIONS

Please remember that the tips, advice and techniques I am about to share with you are meant as guiding ideas only and not as rules. One of the many popular, and true opinions of swinging is that there is no right or wrong way to go about it. So, whether this is your first time swinging or not, I am simply inviting you to discover the SAFE Strategy. What you choose to take from it and apply to your individual swing style will remain entirely at your discretion.

Be prepared for the relevance of each technique or tip we encounter to change with every new swing contract. Before swinging a new production, it might always be worth returning to this book to evaluate which ideas could still be useful, may no longer be useful or have become newly useful.

Lastly, the teachings of *How to Swing in Musical Theatre* are not gender specific. Performers will therefore be referred to throughout using the pronouns, they, them and theirs.

At the end of this chapter, you should be able to:

- ❏ Confidently define Cut-show, Ingredients, Split-track, Swing Bible, Template Track and Variables.
- ❏ Name the SAFE Strategy as a swing method.
- ❏ Explain how the SAFE Strategy divides the swing workload into two categories.
- ❏ Describe a methodical approach to making a swing bible.
- ❏ Use this book to conceive, re-evaluate or specifically advise your swing method.

4. SUCCESS BEFORE YOU BEGIN

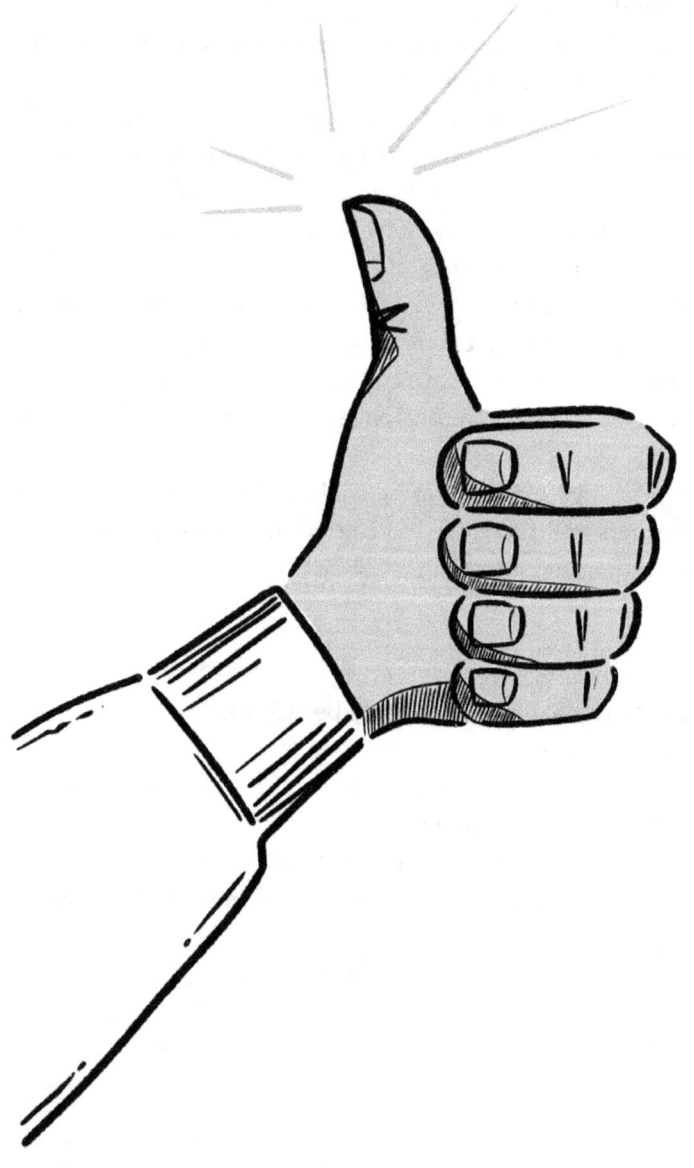

Four
Success before you begin

If swinging well, spotting a swing from an ensemble cast member on stage should be impossible. But linger outside a West End stage door as cast members begin their commute home and spotting swings can be as easy as spotting the people underneath the heftier rucksacks. In fact, one of my favourite production managers in the business has long since enjoyed calling me a turtle because of 'the house' I used to carry on my back as a swing.

> PRODUCTION MANAGER: Overseer of technical elements of a show co-ordinating with producers, designers and show crew to ensure productions are set up safely, on time and within budget.

It doesn't need to be a rucksack per se (though rucksacks do offer certain postural advantages) but on what you should keep inside, that I can confidently advise.

WHAT'S INSIDE A SWING'S RUCKSACK?

Script & score

Before a performer starts a contract, they will be contacted by their company manager regarding any need-to-know information such as rehearsal location, prior costume fittings and their call-time for the first day. This is also an opportune moment for swings to ask about the delivery of the script and score.

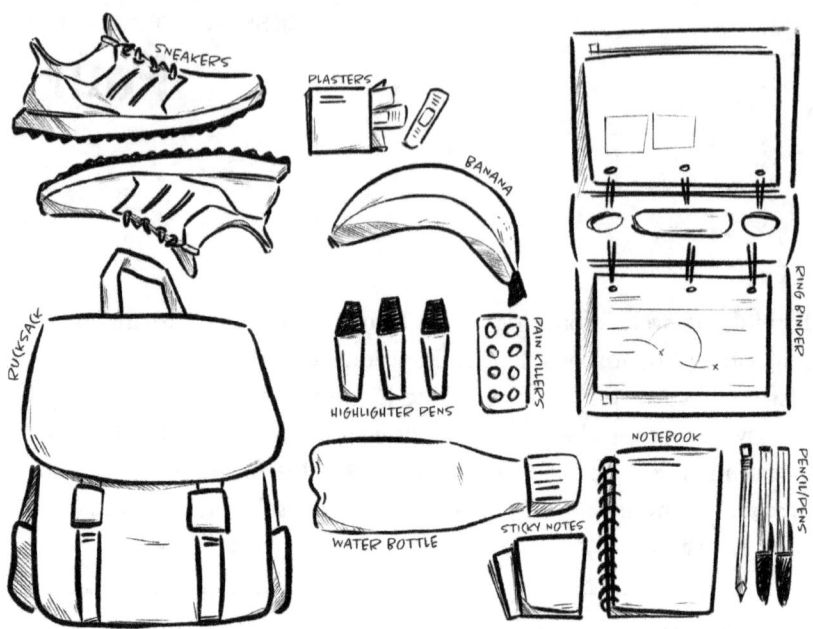

Figure 4.1 What's inside a swing's rucksack?

Swings are encouraged to seek both digital and hard copies to maximise their ongoing options. Where hard copies are yet to be printed and bound, you might request your copy to be:

- Printed single-sided to allow the reverse side to be used for additional notetaking.
- Unbound to make it easier when later organising notes into a swing bible.
- Bound because it can be easier to handle in the early stages of rehearsal.

It is likely that through the audition process a swing will have done their fair share of research into the show concerned. Since they arguably have the most to learn, continued familiarisation with the show ahead of the first day of rehearsals is recommended. Listening to cast recordings and watching available video material are both great ways to help embed melodies and the order of plot events. Once in possession of a script and score, swings can also memorise the lines of any small parts they suspect will be played by the ensemble cast.

Pencil case

A day at work without a pencil case as a swing can feel as fatal as a footballer leaving their boots at home. While no limits can be placed on its contents (much to the delight of all stationery lovers), a few essential items should be named.

Pencil & separate eraser

For most, taking rough notes in pencil before writing up neat notes in pen is a natural progression. It is a practice that was likely instilled from a young age in school but be warned, nothing in theatre is permanent, absolutely nothing.

Figure 4.2 E-Principle

Whether rough or neat, swing notes should always be written in pencil simply because it is easier to erase when things change. To that point, now would be a good time to suggest investing in a quality eraser too.

Coloured pens/pencils/highlighters

Coloured writing instruments have their advantages when swinging, but many swings find they use them less than they expect to.

Again, to avoid difficulty erasing information, the use of colour when notetaking is discouraged. It is also good practice to make the following considerations before using it:

    a) Can I record or present this information just as clearly without using colour?

    b) If I use colour, how time-consuming would the correction job be if the information recorded were to change?

How to Swing in Musical Theatre will prove that though the use of colour is a useful tool, it is not a necessity to swing effectively.

Ruler

Lines are everywhere in theatre: Performers stand in rows, a centre line divides the stage, set moves in linear directions. Put simply, rulers are a swing must-have.

Notebook

Swings will primarily use their notebook(s) to scribble variables at speed during a rehearsal process. Popular considerations when choosing a suitable notebook include size, page layout and binding.

Size

Swings need only avoid notebooks that are impractically small. As a consensus, any equivalent of an A5 notebook or larger is preferred.

Page layout

Swing notes will include a mixture of written notes and sketches. Blank, dotted or ruled pages are therefore recommended over squared or graph paper to avoid overcrowded pages.

Binding

Fragile spines, such as spiral bound notebooks, have been known to cost swings time and energy replacing lost notes. Swings should therefore be mindful to pick a hardwearing notebook that can withstand the daily wear and tear it will be subject to.

Ring binder

The documentation which makes up a swing bible can be incredibly varied. A ring binder is the perfect place to collate it all in an orderly fashion, interspersing diagrams with excerpts of script and other useful documentation.

Swings use document wallets to protect the essential information that goes into their swing bibles and dividers to promote user-friendliness. As a pro tip, document wallets make the page wider than you think so invest in extra-wide dividers to match.

Notecards

Notecards are not considered essential kit to swing but many swings find smaller, A6 or similar, cards particularly useful once a show is up and running for quick reference notes about specific tracks. If you have enjoyed using notecards before now (i.e., to revise for an examination or deliver a presentation), you will likely enjoy using them to swing.

Video recording device

Some, but not all, rehearsal rooms allow swings to record rehearsal footage. Where this is made possible, make sure your device is readily charged and has sufficient memory available.

A BLUEPRINT

A blueprint is a bird's eye depiction of the stage or playing space. Ideally, it is drawn to scale and sets out the location of performer entrances and exits.

To appreciate the bigger picture at their earliest opportunity, swings should seek a technical drawing of the stage, hereafter a 'blueprint', as soon as possible.

Swings might want to think ahead and ask the company manager for an available electronic blueprint at the same time as asking about the delivery of their script and score. If a blueprint cannot be secured in advance, which is not uncommon, the company manager and dance captain are both appropriate points of contact to approach once rehearsals begin.

Sometimes, difficulty sourcing a technical drawing in advance can force a swing to make do for a time with a hand drawn blueprint of their own. They can do this based on:

1. The rehearsal room mark-up.
2. Available images of the set.
3. A model of the set.

> MARK-UP: An outline, often taped, of the set dimensions on the rehearsal room floor.

At the start of a rehearsal process, it is common for the set designer to spend some time introducing the company to the set using sketches, computer generated imagery or perhaps a set model. It is an exciting moment for everyone involved because it is representative of all the hard work done by the creative team to arrive at the first stages of full company rehearsal.

The electronic blueprint you are supplied with will likely include details, such as overhead bars which hang lights and backdrops, that are unnecessary for swing purposes and only serve to crowd the image. A practical blueprint will reflect the most basic interpretation of the playing space (inclusive of entrances and exits), so that it has maximal capacity to have information added to it by swings.

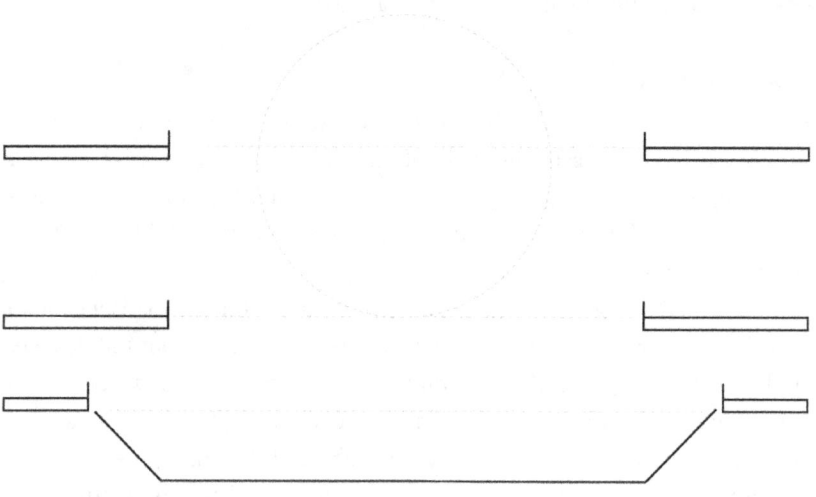

Figure 4.3 An example blueprint

Luckily, we are now swinging in a day and age where computer programs and apps make it easier for the average swing to "clean up" a busy blueprint. If a swing doesn't feel confident to do so digitally, there is no clean up job too big for a pot of correction fluid and a photocopier.

Part of what makes sourcing a blueprint so essential for swings lies in the versatile ways it can assist their process. Most notably, swings will neatly transfer their rehearsal room notes concerning the geography of tracks onto a blueprint to create swing maps.

> SWING MAP: A pictorial representation of the state of play on stage, from a bird's eye view, notably demonstrating the whereabouts of tracks and set pieces.

If a swing bible were like our flipbook animation from before, each swing map would be the equivalent of one illustration.

That said, a blueprint can also be used much earlier in the swing process to record variables at speed in the rehearsal room. Practically, it is both quicker and more accurate to jot down a formation directly onto a blueprint than it is a blank page in a notebook. In fact, a swing in rehearsal might find themselves reaching for a blueprint more regularly than their notebook. It is therefore a good idea to keep a constant, plentiful supply of blueprints by photocopying whatever version you can get your hands on, be that your own sketch or a technical drawing.

FINAL PREPARATIONS

It is the eve of your first day of rehearsals and, following wise advice from your childhood, you have packed your rucksack the night before. There is just one final piece of preparation you might like to do before trying to get a good night's sleep despite all the adrenaline of starting a new job.

A swing will miss information during the rehearsal process for any number of honest reasons such as needing to forego one conversation to hear another or leave the rehearsal room entirely to attend a costume fitting. SAFE swings try to learn the ingredients while recording the variables at the same time and such a constant state of multitasking causes information to slip through the cracks. If it were possible to pack an extra pair of eyes and ears into our rucksacks, I would not hesitate to insist on it.

But this warning is not meant to scare you, instead it wants to assure you that it is perfectly normal for swings not to know everything, all of the time, if not inevitable. Non-swings can also contribute to a supportive working environment by letting go of any expectation that swings should be immediately all-knowing.

Of course, while the expectation to know everything might be an impossible ask, it is certainly a praiseworthy goal to work towards. When working as a swing, I loved getting as close as possible to being omniscient by keeping an up-to-date list of what I didn't know. Call me romantic but I always thought 'so long as I am aware of what I don't know, I know everything I need to know'.

I called it my 'I don't know' list and it would live on the back page of my notebook. In the rehearsal room, as soon as I suspected information to have slipped my attention, I did not panic, I just added a bullet point on my 'I don't know' list.

I have known items on my list to have been as cumbersome as needing to learn whole musical numbers or as small as needing to check where the brakes were on a table. The trick to safe and efficient swinging is that no missed detail is too small to disqualify it from being listed on an 'I don't know' list.

Tea breaks and rehearsal calls that do not use the full cast are an ideal time for swings to scan the room for anyone available that might be able to help provide answers to their list of unknowns. Of course, to be useful, an 'I don't know' list needs to be managed well. It is just as important to add items to the list as it is to delete them as soon as they have been resolved.

> Keeping a list of what you don't know as a swing is an act of self-sufficiency that is particularly valued by resident creative teams who will be too busy to monitor rehearsal oversights per individual swing.

Time permitting, before stepping in for an absent track, a swing can consult their 'I don't know' list to double check for any relevant gaps in their knowledge that could potentially stop the rehearsal, or worse the show, due to compromised function or safety.

Figure 4.4 F-Principle

Figure 4.5 S-Principle

The purpose of an 'I don't know' list is therefore two-fold: first, it helps to alleviate unnecessary stress that comes from an impatient need to know everything as soon as it is taught and second, it can be used as a final checklist before swinging to ensure overall show function and safety.

Ahead of the first day of rehearsals then, a swing prepped for success will have already written 'I don't know...' as a title in the back of their hardwearing notebook.

At the end of this chapter, you should be able to:

❑ List what items a swing might need to perform effectively.
❑ Suggest ways a swing can prepare in advance of a rehearsal process.
❑ Describe what a blueprint is and explain what it might be used for.
❑ Confidently define Mark-up, Production Manager and Swing Map.

5. HOW TO LEARN THE INGREDIENTS

How to learn the ingredients

Five

Many performers develop their swing skills unconsciously long before they are offered their first professional swing contract. Practice can be seen as early as in the bright and helpful talent attending youth theatre groups. As rehearsals and productions are plagued by students falling ill, or worse – dropping out of performances entirely – a handful of helpful young minds, or 'baby swings', will likely throw their hat into the ring to mend the damage. They might volunteer to dance with a new partner or switch harmony lines to help with the vocal balance. To baby swings, it's innocently doing what is necessary; to their teachers it's a great sigh of relief; to musical theatre, it's swinging.

The terms ingredients and track might still be new to you, but you have probably experienced what it is to learn the ingredients of an ensemble track before. To perform in a musical without needing to write anything down, is in fact to learn the ingredients of an ensemble track by simply getting up and practicing them. Suddenly, the saying 'practice makes perfect' rings remarkably true.

In all the excitement of buying a new pencil case, swings can easily forget that they know how to learn ingredients through physical practice and instead try to learn them by sitting behind a desk and writing. If this were a good idea, we should probably start teaching dance and drama in classrooms not studios.

Hurrah, being a swing does not mean you need to rethink your approach to performing. In fact, 50% of your total swing workload, learning the ingredients, involves doing as you have always done, getting up and practicing.

WHY THE BODY STORES THE INGREDIENTS

Many performers will resonate with the adrenaline-fuelled experience of being saved by their body at the very moment their minds go blank. You might have experienced the correct lyric magically rolling off your tongue or your legs automatically dancing the right steps. Common

DOI: 10.4324/9781003254300-6

causes of apparent mind blanking include nervousness, stress and too many thoughts running through your head, all three of which are no stranger to swings.

Even when show conditions are calm, never-before worn costumes, never-before-used props and never-before-experienced lighting states can startle swings into total mind blank. Those that can rely on their muscle memory to kick in with the ingredients are more available to cope with each new challenge as it is met (often live on stage and in front of a paying audience).

Ensemble performers are spoiled with time to drill *what* they do (AKA their ingredients) into their bodies whereas swings are not given the same frequency of opportunity. To compensate, swings make use of space on the side-lines of a rehearsal room to gain the volume of practice they need to develop a muscle memory for the ingredients.

> Perceptive swings recognise when it is inappropriate to practice alongside the main rehearsal. The creative lead in the room might, for example, need to reflect on their work without surplus bodies in their periphery. Alternatively, you might spot that an onstage cast member is feeling flustered and pause practicing to enable calmer surroundings for them.

CHOOSING WHICH INGREDIENTS TO PRACTICE

If you are a performer reading this, you probably have experience of using repetitive practice to learn the ingredients of one track. Swings however must learn multiple versions of the ingredients in the form of multiple tracks. If they were to practice every possible version of the ingredients, they might not have time for any repetitive practice at all. SAFE swings rise to this challenge by doing as the ensemble do, repetitively practicing the ingredients of just one track; their template track.

To recap, a template track is a hypothetical track made up of common ingredients between ensemble tracks so that it bears the most resemblance to them all. In addition to helping swings develop a muscle memory for a standard version of ingredients, a well-constructed template track enables them to maintain rehearsal momentum by using it to step into any track, at any time, with reasonable accuracy. To make this possible, it is best to construct a template track in chunks. Some chunks will be a carbon copy of what another track does (namely the one that has the most in common with others) while other chunks will be hypothetical, conceived by the swing to reflect what most tracks are doing for a given time.

For want of a swing hack to spot what makes a good hypothetical chunk, imagine a choreographer teaching a section of choreography which will be danced facing multiple directions. If they teach the variables first, each track would try to learn the choreography facing a different direction. A fine choice for an ensemble cast with eyes on the back of their heads. Far more practically, they might teach what all tracks have in common (hereafter 'common ingredients') facing a universal "front" first, before allocating each track a different direction to face.

As demonstrated by this example, most scenarios enable choreographers to teach common ingredients first and play with variables after, which is a really useful order of events for swings to recognise. Often, the first version of the ingredients taught to an ensemble (likely when the whole room is still facing a mirror) is appropriate for use as a hypothetical chunk of ingredients. Upon repetitive practice of this chunk, they will successfully rehearse a portion of their template track into their bodies.

> The development of a template track also helps to sustain rehearsal momentum in a secondary capacity since, if needed to step in, it is quicker to teach an unsure swing *where* to be than it is to teach them *what* to do.

ALL VARIABLES AND NO INGREDIENTS

From time to time, when all tracks are performing wildly different ingredients, a swing may need to abandon the idea of a template track and instead learn what each track does separately. This is the common case when creatives use rehearsal time to create busy scenes, workshop ideas or perhaps, ask the cast to improvise. Invariably, these will be the moments that are less familiar in the body and hence swings may need to revise them before a performance, but they needn't cause you to sit down in the rehearsal room.

When productions move to the performance venue the opportunity for swings to get up and practice plummets. So, to stand a chance at developing your most powerful muscle memory, do not delay, **get up and practice whenever you can because the luxury of being able to will not last forever.**

Here are some productive ways you can take advantage of the chance to be on your feet in the rehearsal room even when there are no obvious template ingredients to practice.

Option 1: Learn what the small majority does

Even if the majority is only won by a single track, the odds support that it is this version of the ingredients you are going to need to know first, so why not learn it?

Option 2: Learn as a team of swings

If your swing team are up for it, you might decide to divide tracks between you in order to conquer them all. Simply allocate each swing a track to focus on and arrange to share what you learn later.

Option 3: Learn One-Track-At-A-Time

Take your pick of the tracks and learn what they do. Time spent on your feet is always better than not getting up at all but note that you can make an informed choice about which track you practice. For example, do you know if a particular track is due to leave for a wig fitting any time soon? Are some ensemble members more helpful than others when you have questions about their track? Does one track appear more intricate than another?

This is the only scenario in which I can endorse a One-Track-At-A-Time Strategy for swinging. To avoid getting trapped in a state of tunnel vision, aspire to recognise when the smallest majority returns to the rehearsal room and recommence practicing those ingredients as part of your template track.

REHEARSING INGREDIENTS IN FORMATION

A template track is like the backbone from which all tracks stem but differ ever so slightly. Whenever information across ensemble tracks differs from it, a variable is in play which must be recorded. Common variables include:

- Position
- Counts
- Direction
- Use of opposition

Position, meaning where one track is placed in the playing space, is the one variable that is likely to trick swings who rely on ingredients being taught first. Sometimes a cast will be placed in a formation before ingredients are taught. It therefore needs to become force of habit that whenever an ensemble changes formation, a swing jots down the new position of each track.

> Some swing and ensemble performers, find it helpful to learn the ingredients by writing the choreography out in longhand outside of rehearsal time. You might suppose this method contradicts any ruling that says ingredients are strictly remembered and only variables are recorded. In this context, the purpose of writing the ingredients is to enable the performer to remember them eventually and you too are encouraged to embrace whatever learning style you find helpful to meet that aim. The important point to recognise is that, at some point, all performers, whether swing or ensemble, aspire to throw away any notes they have about ingredients.

BEWARE OF THE MINIMAL CAST CHANGE

A minimal cast change is defined by less cast members joining a company than are leaving. This could happen at the point of contract renewal or mid production run if, for example, additional or replacement hires are made.

Imagine a rehearsal process for a minimal cast change in which you are a swing, alongside three new ensemble performers out of twelve ensemble tracks. Since the continuing company will have to juggle both rehearsals and their regular performance schedule, the joining cast will likely start learning the show without them. As the swing, you are now faced with observing a rehearsal room that represents just a fraction of the bigger picture which is bad news for those wanting to spot common ingredients for a template track.

Since the show itself pre-exists, ensemble tracks might also be taught to a swing as they appear in the show, that is with variables already applied. So, the assurance that the ingredients will be taught first, and the variables applied later flies out the window. Working backwards to extract the ingredients you need for your template track could be as hard as trying to work out what the joke was when you are only given the punch line.

It is not impossible though and certainly with early consideration of their circumstance, swings can prepare themselves for success. Primarily, they can take advantage of an increased opportunity to ask questions while there are less bodies in the rehearsal room. Constructive questions sound like:

'What does the overall pattern look like?'
'Is that a set choice or is there room for interpretation?'
'What version do most of the ensemble do?'

With so many gaps in the rehearsal room, it is also the perfect opportunity for a swing to get up and practice. While that might reduce time available to record variables, it does provide an opportunity for a swing to work a version of the ingredients into their muscle memory. Working in this way is a very similar experience to working as an onstage swing.

The best advice I can offer swings rehearsing separately from the total onstage cast is that patience will need to be your best friend. The number of times you hear the wonderful phrase 'it will make more sense when the full company joins us' will only serve to prove me right on that front.

HARMONIES: INGREDIENT OR VARIABLE?

In case swinging was not hard enough, swings must learn the vocal harmonies of each track they cover. Given the idea that ingredients are recalled from memory, you might assume vocal harmonies fall neatly into this category too. Depending on the expectation of the production concerned however, drawing a hard and fast line on this debate is not so easy.

In a vocal call, a musical director will often allocate each swing a primary harmony line so that the overall sound made in the rehearsal room is balanced. For example, a team of two female swings might rehearse as one alto voice and one soprano voice. Of course, the neatness of this set up would be overthrown if ever the vocal arrangements split into three parts or more.

Alternatively, if your team of swings have been given their cover allocations, it is a good idea to rehearse the harmony line sung by most of the tracks you are first in line to cover.

Irrespective of how it is decided which line you will sing in the rehearsal room; you will probably embed one as a default line and record the others for later learning. If we apply SAFE terminology to this approach, swings embed a *template* harmony line (their vocal *ingredients*) into their muscle memory and keep audio recordings of variable harmony lines (their vocal *variables*).

On some productions, swings can sing their template harmony line for any track they perform without a significant effect to the ensemble sound. When a notable number of ensemble absences accumulate, swings might be asked to switch harmony lines to remedy the vocal balance. This is a relaxed approach swinging harmonies, and while it is not unusual, it should not be expected.

In musical numbers that heavily integrate singing and dancing, the difficulty of singing different notes while dancing the same steps cannot be underestimated. Yet another reason why swings embed all other ingredients in their muscle memory is so that they free mental space to sing a less familiar harmony line when needed.

That said, the voice is also a muscle and so in reverse, you may find it just as beneficial to develop a muscle memory for each vocal line to concentrate on dancing less familiar steps.

Whether you view vocal harmonies as an ingredient or a variable, we can all accept this blanket rule for learning them in the rehearsal room:

Record it all so that you can perform it all... eventually.

Of the minor mistakes a swing might make, they will often cover up the physical ones by doing what the industry calls 'styling it out'. Minor audible mistakes, especially in exposed vocal moments, can be far less forgiving and so swings must not misjudge the value of securing their vocal harmonies.

THE SAFE STRATEGY FOR LEARNING INGREDIENTS

SAFE swings start learning the ingredients by getting up and practicing their template track. The advantages are that:

1. They embrace any pre-existing skill of learning by doing.
2. The body acts as an insurance policy for mind blanking.
3. Trusting the body to remember the ingredients maximises the mental availability of swings to respond to changing show conditions.

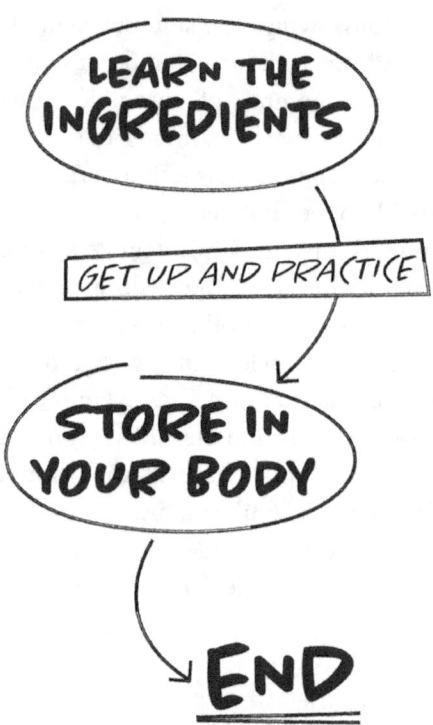

Figure 5.1 The SAFE Strategy: How to learn the ingredients

Once they trust their body to remember their template track, swings must continue to practice any additional ingredients they were unable to include in it. This is likely owing to times when two or more tracks are doing remarkably different things.

At the end of this chapter, you should be able to:

❑ Understand that ingredients are learnt by getting up and practicing.
❑ Explain the importance of storing the ingredients in the body.
❑ Share ideas on how to identify common ingredients and construct a template track.
❑ Maintain the momentum of a rehearsal using your template track.
❑ Discuss the challenges associated with rehearsing for a minimal cast change as a swing.
❑ Comment on the classification of vocal harmonies as an ingredient or a variable.
❑ Understand what is meant by the SAFE Strategy for learning the ingredients.

6. HOW TO RECORD THE VARIABLES

Six

How to record the variables

All variables that a swing does not trust themselves to remember, typically position, counts, use of opposition, direction and traffic, must be recorded for safe keeping.

> TRAFFIC: A variable describing the pathway a track takes between two stationary positions.

Variables are often first scribbled at speed in the rehearsal room by the swing whose main priorities are practicing the ingredients of a template track and keeping their eyes on the unfolding rehearsal in front of them.

Swings limit their time spent writing by limiting the nature of what they choose to record. Holding a useful mantra close, such as 'record where and when (the variables) not what (the ingredients)', helps to limit the risk of writing in excess.

Figure 6.1 Record where and when, not what

DOI: 10.4324/9781003254300-7

Nonetheless, when thrown a lot of information in a small amount of time, swings can struggle to be picky about what they do or do not record – even the most experienced swings still scribble a few ingredients here or there.

Fortunately, the rehearsal process represents just the beginning of an entire production process and so swings will have ample opportunity in the future to scale back rehearsal notes to what is necessary. In fact, we will learn that the recording of variables, from rehearsal room to swing bible, is a three-step process:

Step 1: Get it down.
Step 2: Scale it down.
Step 3: Write it up.

Thanks to this assurance, I was always able to find comfort in the following advice offered to me by a fellow swing:

'No one will tell you what to learn or when to learn it but if it's all written down, your body and your brain can relax'.

LONG-LIFE REHEARSAL NOTES

It is common for the need to record variables quickly to result in completely illegible rehearsal notes. Fearing that the same notes won't make sense for much longer, swings stress about copying them up "in neat" as soon as possible and often forego rest in favour of doing so. Swings are more able to create downtime for themselves when their rehearsal notes are clearly recorded and well organised. Even wiser advice from that fellow swing might therefore have sounded like:

'No one will tell you what to learn or when to learn it but if it's all written down [and you can understand what you have written], your body and your brain can relax.'

First then, there are a few housekeeping rules we can stick to when formatting rehearsal notes so swings can trust they will understand theirs for longer. Second, we will learn some basics of swing notation (Chapter 7) to help you to write as much as possible, clearly and in as few scrawls as possible.

Rule 1: Title your work

In life we are often indebted to labels (for one thing, they help us to use sugar instead of salt in our tea). You would be surprised at how many swings forget to label their rehearsal notes due to their haste when recording variables.

The irony is, swings waste more time deciphering what untitled rehearsal notes mean than if they had jotted one down in the first place.

Deciding on a title is an instinctive process, simply say what you see. Some sensible examples include:

- Dance break
- First verse
- Scene change
- Bouquet catch

> It might be worth syncing up your titles with your dance captain and/or fellow swings. The more a team uses the same language, the easier it is to share and compare notes without confusion. Pre-existing shows often have a library of amusing nicknames for different sections of a show. Keep an ear out for common show lingo to speak the same language and for your sheer amusement.

Rule 2: Add a page number

Swings might always hope to turn to the next available blank page in their notebooks, but the reality of the rehearsal room is that sometimes, any page (and any orientation for that matter) will do. As a result, rehearsal notes easily fall out of sequence, causing stress, worry, confusion and wasted time that might have easily been avoided with the provision of a page number.

Rule 3: Add a date or time

If rehearsing a show in creation, rehearsal rooms are subject to constant change; one minute it is this formation, the next minute it is that formation. Dates, therefore, help swings to identify the most up-to-date and relevant information from their rehearsal notes. If things changed a lot in the space of a day, I would sometimes go so far as to add a time to my page.

Rule 4: Mark where downstage is

Downstage is the theatrical term for the area of playing space at the front of the stage, situated closest to the audience. It is worth noting that different types of stage, such as *traverse* and *in the round*, can make downstage difficult to identify.

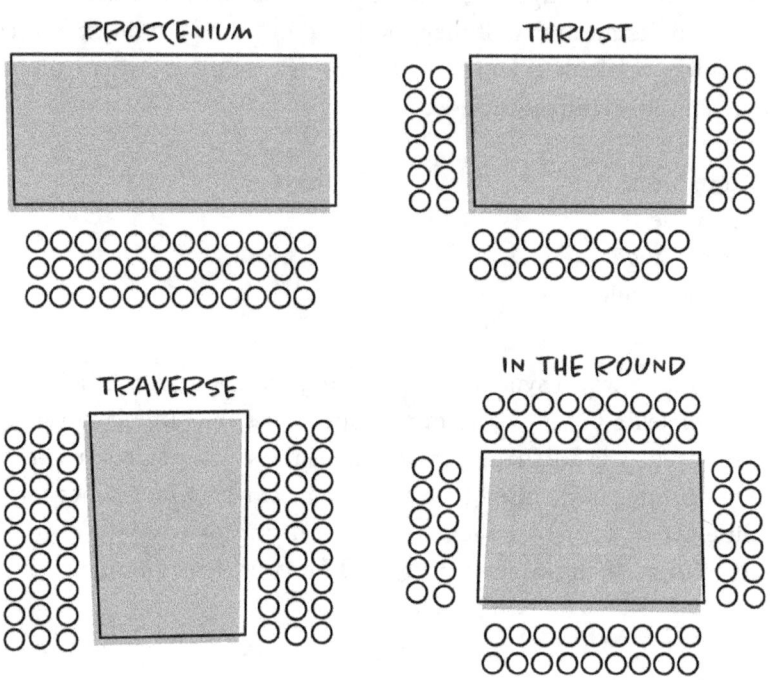

Figure 6.2 Types of stage

Swings will record multiple formations during the rehearsal process, which will later be used to create swing maps. To save themselves future confusion, a mark specifying 'DS' for downstage should be placed demonstratively on each formation to know how it should be viewed with confidence. Interpreting a formation without a downstage mark is a lot like interpreting a road map that fails to tell you where north is.

> Proscenium Arch describes the framework that separates the stage from the audience in most end-on theatres. Interestingly, when we break the term down, it is the framework (arch) that sits in front of (pro) the scene (scenium).

Rule 5: Draw a centre line

When drawing formations at speed, drawing to scale is bound to suffer or be disregarded entirely. For example, you might hurriedly sketch stage left using a larger scale than stage right meaning the tracks on stage left appear further apart. Without a centre line, when you later revisit the same map, the tracks will probably look a bit askew. Remember to draw a centre line on your maps so that, at the very least, you will know which tracks are positioned on stage right and stage left.

Rule 6: Describe stage width

As a performer, to be asked, 'Are you on your number?', means to ask, 'Are you positioned at accurate width?'

> STAGE NUMBERS: A graduated measure of stage width used to accurately position performers and maintain formation over time. Commonly marked discreetly along the downstage edge of the show floor. Zero equates to centre and numbers ascend moving outward.

Moving incrementally outwards of centre, it is common theatrical practice for productions to place markers, referred to as 'stage numbers', at the front of the stage. It is a way of making sure formations are both accurate and consistent.

In the UK, stage numbers usually ascend by two for every two feet moving out from centre where centre is represented by zero.

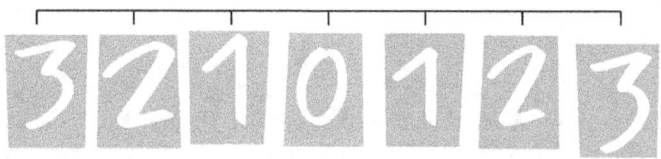

Figure 6.3 Stage numbers

> The scaling of stage numbers varies on different productions. In ballet, quarter and eighth marks are used to divide the stage into proportionate segments as their names would suggest. To be discreet, some productions build evenly spaced LED lights into their show floor, though, at the time of writing, stage numbers are more frequently used to graduate width.

Over time, ensemble members will wean themselves from the need to look down and check that they are standing on the correct number. Through repetition, their bodies start to remember how far away they are positioned from other people or set pieces. Unable to compete with the same level of familiarity, swings record the stage numbers of tracks in the rehearsal room to later be able to accurately place themselves on stage.

Recording stage numbers needs to be a knee-jerk reaction of swings. As a nicety, and by no means guarantee, some choreographers will check in with the swing team before they begin creating a subsequent formation. When working with a team of effective swings however, the answer to the choreographer's question 'swings, can I move on?' will always be a resounding, 'yes'.

To record stage numbers at speed and with necessary accuracy, swings draw a number rule at the base or top of any sketch that records where tracks are as a minimum requirement.

MINIMUM PRESENTATION CHECKLIST

Collating our housekeeping rules, the following minimum presentation checklist can be used to annotate your long-life rehearsal notes:

1. A title
2. A page number
3. A date
4. A DS mark
5. A centre line
6. A width descriptor

> Some may question the need for both a DS mark and a width descriptor as a minimum requirement. Surely the position of a number rule on the page can also indicate where downstage is?
>
> There will be times when swings must scribble a formation on whatever piece of paper they can find. At one time or another, the back of a receipt from my wallet was not off limits. Unless you can guarantee a **consistent** position for your every number rule, the practice of writing 'DS' on **every** diagram you sketch is moreover a quick and harmless habit to develop that rules out the slightest possibility of confusion later.

When our minimum presentation checklist is satisfied as a matter of habit, swings can be assured their understanding of what they have recorded will not expire, which is essential for affording them the confidence to switch off outside of rehearsal hours.

Every change of formation invites a new swing map to be drawn and labelled with the minimum presentation checklist. Any additional variables that apply while in that formation, for example specific timing or use of opposition, are typically recorded somewhere in the vicinity of the respective swing map.

On average, stage numbers can range anywhere from 8 to 20 places either side of centre. Drawing a scale of that size for every new formation is both tedious and time-consuming.

It is more convenient for swings to draw a number rule on their original blueprint of the playing space before photocopying a supply for rehearsals. Not only do prepared blueprints help to reduce the time a swing spends writing but they also improve accuracy since a photocopied blueprint can be drawn to scale. If swings do use blueprints to record variables in the rehearsal room however, they should note the increased importance of numbering each loose page (item two on the minimum presentation checklist) to protect their composure.

A completed blueprint ready for photocopying needn't just save you time drawing a number scale. You can also include the centre line, DS mark and deliberate empty fields that remind you to complete the remainder of your minimum presentation checklist.

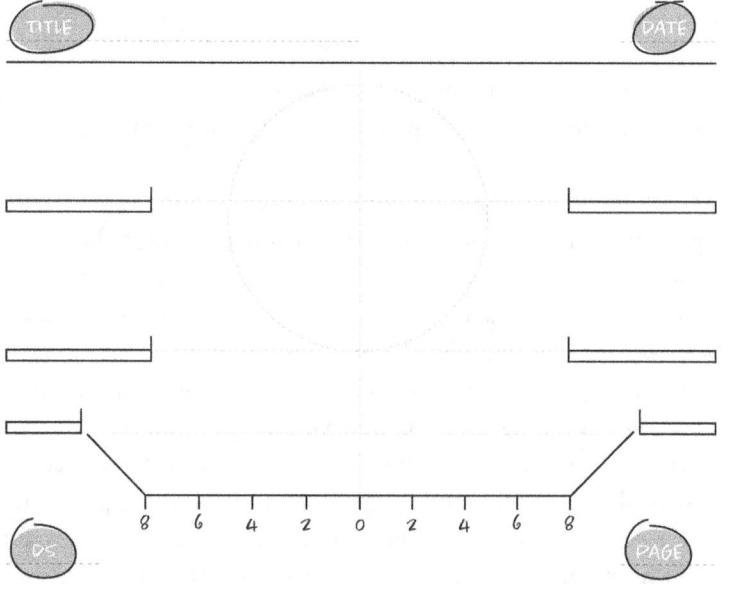

Figure 6.4 An example rehearsal blueprint

As an alternative to blueprints but at the expense of their personal time, swings can prep their notebook pages with hand drawn number rules so that they are readily available to record formation at speed.

REHEARSAL ROOM PRIORITY

A fellow swing once showed me a diagram of an arrow beginning at point A and finishing at point B. 'What's more important?' they asked, 'knowing *what* I'm doing at points A and B or knowing *how* I get from point A to point B?' The same question can be rephrased as 'should I prioritise knowledge of the ingredients or the variables?'

Figure 6.5 How to swing from A to B

With every emphasis so far placed on enabling swings to get up and practice, it would be fair to assume that swings prioritise the ingredients. After all, that would be to:

- Best protect the momentum of a rehearsal.
- Take advantage of practical space to develop muscle memory.

Sometimes however, a variable such as chaotic traffic can destroy the theory that swings should prioritise learning the ingredients in the rehearsal room. Without appropriate knowledge of traffic, the rehearsal room could grind to a halt, even if the ingredients are known intrinsically well, because the risk of collision is too high.

When lots of tracks are performing different ingredients at the same time, again a swing might ensure the continued safe and smooth running of the rehearsal room by prioritising *where* tracks are over *what* they are doing.

Here we have ourselves two scenarios (and there are plenty more) in which prioritising the variables better enables swings to maintain rehearsal momentum or, put simply, serve function. So, to our puzzled swing who was not sure whether to prioritise the ingredients or the variables, the answer is neither but rather to prioritise function.

Figure 6.6 Quoted F-Principle

To make sure you are always prioritising function, from time to time you should ask yourself 'Can I step in?' When the answer is no, focus on whatever information would make it possible to, even if, on occasion, it is the variables.

> During the studio rehearsal phase, when it feels impossible to know whether learning ingredients or variables best serves function, I would always encourage you to practice the ingredients. Time spent on your feet practicing something will never be wasted time in the rehearsal room unlike time spent sat down supposing there is nothing productive you could be doing.

At the end of this chapter, you should be able to:

❑ Recite the mantra 'Record where and when not what' to take rehearsal notes that pertain almost exclusively to variables.
❑ Confidently define Stage Numbers and Traffic.
❑ Explain the importance of taking long-life rehearsal notes.
❑ List the minimum presentation checklist for formatting long-life rehearsal notes.
❑ Use the question 'Can I step in?' to inform rehearsal room priority.

7. BASICS OF NOTATION

Basics of notation
Seven

Despite a swing's best efforts to format long-life rehearsal notes, when a rehearsal room moves at pace, surely illegible scribbles are made inevitable? This is the case for many swings because their only way to be quick is to sacrifice clarity, which is no use to their peace of mind. To protect the clarity of our notes, we must develop a shorthand which is quick by way of reducing the amount we choose to record, not increasing the speed at which we do so.

The skill of recording variables in a shorthand is a lot like the one you might use to reduce your character count on Twitter to post a single tweet. Your aim is to reduce what you see but not what you can understand from it. In my teens, a single text message had a maximum character count too. The more characters I used, the more single text messages I would accumulate and the more I would ultimately spend. So, if I wanted to make my phone credit last longer, I had to learn to lessen my character count by abbreviating my words. Little did I know how useful this skill would be further down the line, LOL.

An illustrated shorthand can be compared to the way we use emojis today, for example, a simple thumbs up can say many words.

There are many popular ways swings convert what they see in the rehearsal room into a shorthand on paper, some so popular that they make up what we shall know as 'the basics of swing notation'.

HOW TO RECORD WHO TRACKS ARE

On the first day of rehearsals, all departments have a lot to learn. Most will be able to take their time getting to know the names of all the people that make up a company. This is not the luxury of a swing.

Swings record notes about various cast members within minutes of first meeting them. As rehearsals continue, these names will be written repeatedly so, it is a good idea for swings to decipher a shorthand for recording information pertaining to who at their earliest opportunity.

DOI: 10.4324/9781003254300-8

First, you can try and source a cast list; a task made easy thanks to casting announcements on the internet. Why wait for the first day of rehearsals to get to know the names of the people you will be writing about over and over again?

> CODING: The process of abbreviating track names to enable fast notation.

Second, you can start to think about how you will abbreviate or code the names of each performer or track name i.e, character.

Like swinging in general, coding is a very personal process and it is important I assure you that there is no correct way to code, there is only what makes sense to you. That said, I have drawn on my years of experience as a swing to share with you a flowchart (see page 71) which best describes a coding method to fit most musical companies. Once again, the term 'principal role' encompasses supporting roles and other named character parts.

> Where possible I would always try to code principal or character name over the ensemble performer name because given a cast change, character names will remain the same whereas performer names will not.

I invite you to try it out: Take a theatre programme or playbill, follow the flowchart, and derive your abbreviations for that company.

> I highly recommend using the rule of three to code: Abbreviate each track in exactly three letters, even if it can be done in less.
>
> Using more than three letters will take time to scribe and will eventually take up valuable space on your notes as they appear in your swing bible.
>
> Using less than three letters can cause confusion. If any two abbreviations share the same first and second letter, both abbreviations require a third letter to differentiate the two.
>
> Of course, there are times when three letters are unnecessary but rather than make an exception, some swings prefer to stick to the rule of three because of the comfort having a well-defined system brings.

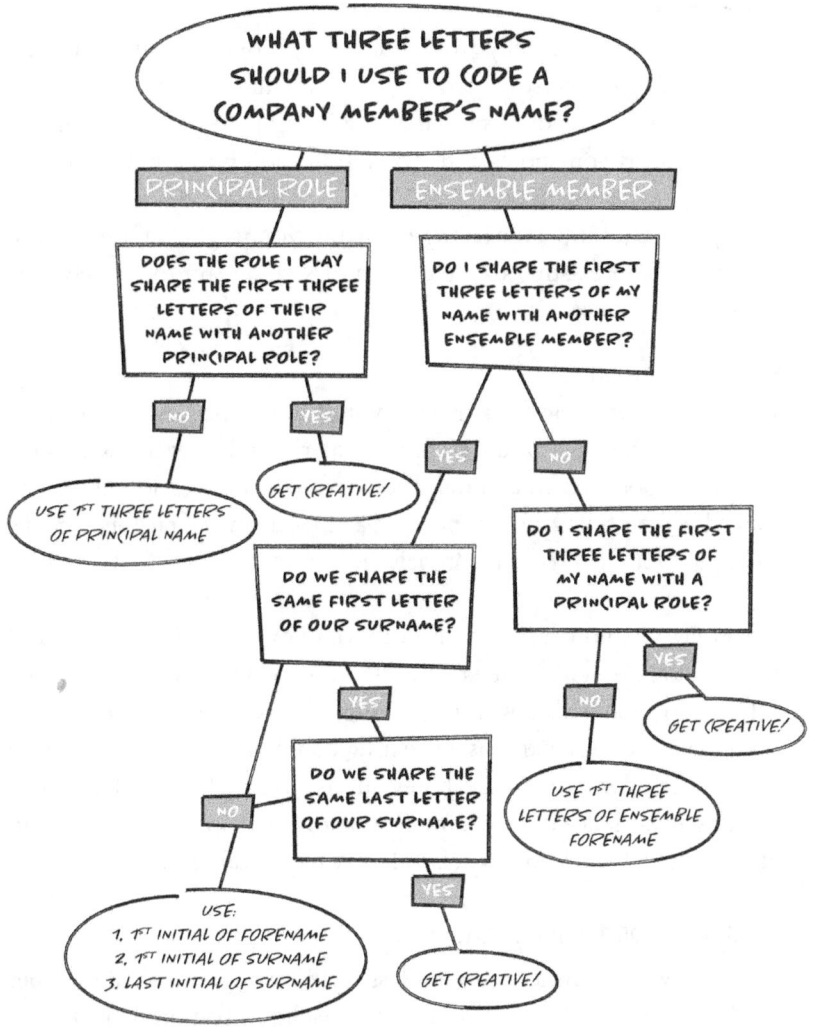

Figure 7.1 A coding method

Things to remember when coding your way are:

1. Consistency.

    When we are consistent, our notes appear clear and organised, hence why we have learnt to consistently satisfy the minimum presentation checklist for every new formation drawn.

    When we are inconsistent, the multiple ways our notes can be interpreted leads to confusion, loss of social hours and stress.

2. Accessibility.
Swings do not commonly work alone; they work as a part of a team. While coding is a personal process, there are undoubted advantages to sharing the same coding system as your teammates. Doing so allows others to read your notes and vice versa, leading to a more efficient working environment.

If you are joining an existing company, you might want to wait to confer with an existing dance captain or swing team to conceive the codes you will use.

3. Speed of translation.
It is a common choice for novice swings to use performer initials to abbreviate the names of tracks. In my experience however, I was much quicker to both record and translate codes when the codes themselves looked as their full names sounded. To abbreviate my name, for example, I would favour 'JAY' over my initials 'JE'.

Hopefully, you now have a clear idea about how you can quickly record information about *who* in the rehearsal room. You will also need to record information about *where*, *when* and *how* ingredients are performed.

Let us start with *where*. Just as texting could have given you existing experience of working with abbreviations, you are likely to have some existing experience of recording formations on paper, we just need to cast our minds back to our schooling years to realise it.

HOW TO RECORD WHERE TRACKS ARE

If there is a way to make swinging less intimidating, it is to remember that it is in fact one of your oldest skills. At school, you probably used x and y axes to draw different types of charts:

- Line graphs
- Scatter graphs
- Pie charts
- Bar charts

Swings awaken their chart drawing skills to accurately record where tracks are positioned on stage. To do this, they need two pieces of information:

1. How far stage right or stage left a track is positioned (x), described by stage numbers or alternative 'width descriptors'.
2. How far upstage or downstage a track is positioned (y), described by set pieces, lighting towers and wings or alternative 'depth descriptors'.

In the absence of stage numbers altogether, all productions will rely on a visual to describe the width of people and set. In such circumstance, swings are encouraged to become acquainted with the positions of noticeable performance space features such as fire exits, speakers, show floor lights, microphones and auditorium aisles, all of which make good practical substitutes for stage numbers.

In swing terms, the process of drawing co-ordinates to represent the position of each track on stage is called 'charting'. The resulting diagram is known as a 'chart' or, more commonly, a 'swing map' and hence the term 'charting' is sometimes used interchangeably with the term 'mapping'. Whenever tracks move into a new formation, swings will 'chart' a new 'swing map'. Visually, they are most similar to scatter graphs.

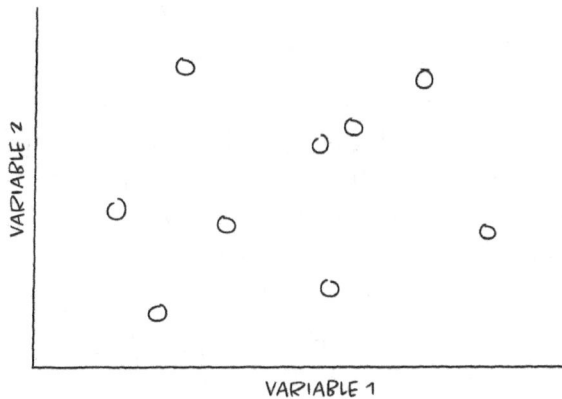

Figure 7.2 Scatter graph

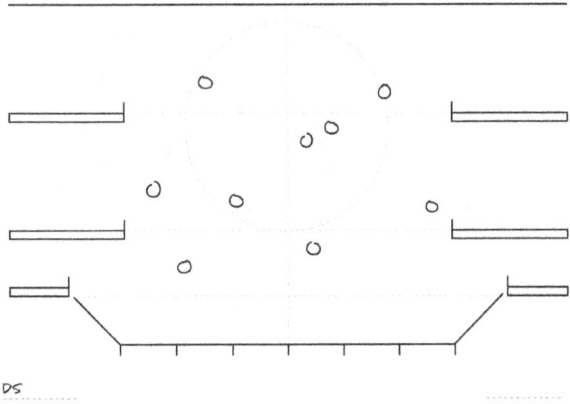

Figure 7.3 A stationary swing map

CROSSHAIRS

It is common practice to use symbols to indicate where a track is positioned. Some swings like to use different symbols to differentiate between tracks they cover, opposite sex tracks and principal roles. Respectively, they might use a ×, a ○ and a □. There is a particular advantage, however, to using crosshairs (×) when charting.

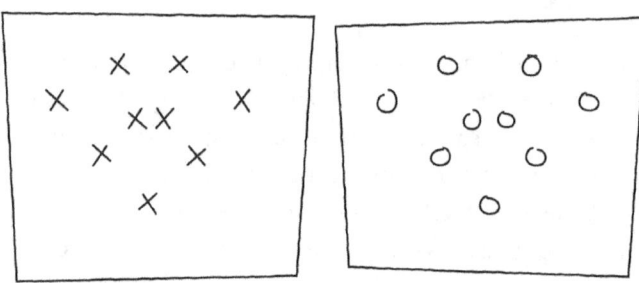

Figure 7.4 Crosshairs vs. basic shapes

Like a battleship using radar to detect rival ships at sea, basic shapes can only provide a general bearing or region in which tracks are positioned. By using crosshairs, the point at which the two lines of the crosshair intersect accurately depicts the exact location of a track. For this reason, to be the most accurate swing, you are advised to favour crosshairs over basic shapes when charting formations.

Swings differentiate each crosshair by simply labelling them, often using their assigned abbreviation or code for each track. Labelling this way keeps swing maps clutter-free. When formations get particularly busy, however, it can become difficult to identify which code belongs to which crosshair as seen by the chaos charted in Figure 7.5.

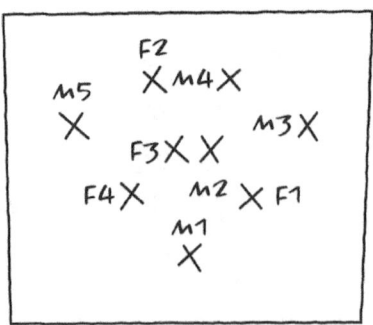

Figure 7.5 Who belongs to which crosshair?

> CHARTING/MAPPING: The technique of plotting the width and depth of tracks as co-ordinates on a bird's eye floorplan of the playing space to produce swing maps.

To maximise accuracy, it is a good idea to create a consistent habit to determine where you will write who each crosshair belongs to. After all, any inconsistency could lead to future deliberation, which will only slow you down. Take a look at the examples provided in Figure 7.6, which do you think would work best for you?

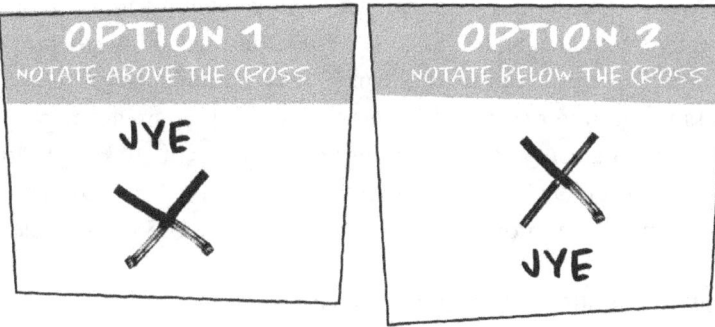

Figure 7.6 Labelling crosshairs

> Sometimes the easiest solution is to make an exception. When exceptions are infrequent, they are useful. When exceptions become frequent, the system ceases to exist and the quality of information recorded is compromised. The key is not to lose sleep over the occasions where you are forced to make an exception but to limit the number of exceptions you allow yourself to make.

Some swings like to allocate each track a colour, for example where Track 6 = Green crosshairs. When using colour, it is not necessary to further label each crosshair. This is particularly useful when there is not enough space on your swing map for your codes.

To satisfy the E-Principle, however, it is important to recognise that colour is difficult to erase. As a result, it is not recommended to use a system of coloured crosshairs while a production is still in creation. Instead, use pencil and stick to consistent labelling habits.

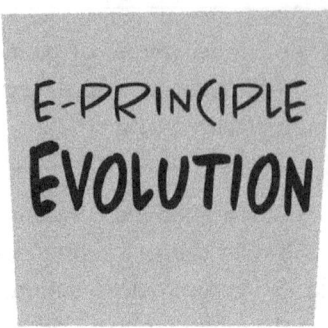

Figure 7.7 E-Principle

Colour is something swings can get excited about using when potential changes to a production look more like soft furnishings than reconstruction. That said, colour can be used at an earlier stage of the swing process if computer software is being used to chart swing maps since the process of erasing colour becomes but a matter of clicking a mouse or tapping a screen. The use of computer software to record variables will be explored in more detail in Chapter 10 – *Ready. Set. Swing bible*.

HOW TO RECORD WHERE TRACKS TRAVEL

Figure 7.8 How to swing from A to B

Remember this conundrum? Swings store what the tracks do at points A and B in their muscle memory. Swings need to record how they move from A to B (record traffic) in their swing bible.

There are three stages to any given journey of a track:

Table 7.1 Three stages of a track journey

Stage 1	Beginning	Beginning position	Stationary map	Where do they begin?
Stage 2	Middle	Traffic	Moving map	What path do they take?
Stage 3	End	Ending position	Stationary map	Where do they end up?

So far, we have learnt how to chart stationary maps showing beginning and ending positions. To turn a stationary map into a moving map, or a middle map showing traffic, we need to learn how to add layers of information.

> LAYER: Pictorial representation of a variable on a stationary map.

Moving maps are stationary maps with the variable of traffic layered on top. Most commonly swings layer traffic using arrows.

ARROWS

Here is a middle map for a circle of eight tracks rotating one space anti-clockwise:

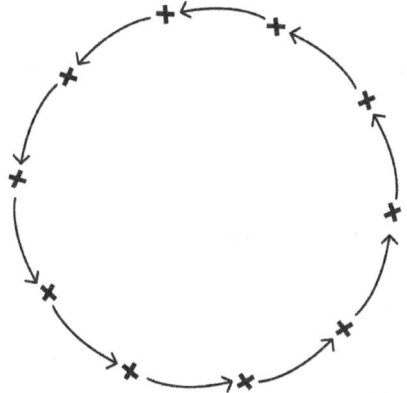

Figure 7.9 Starting position or ending position?

What do these arrows mean to you? Do they show:

a) Where each track will travel to?

or,

b) Where each track has travelled from?

The question might not be so difficult to answer if it were asked immediately after having recorded the information, but wait a week, a month, or more and our level of certainty would nosedive. Swing maps that lose meaning over time create additional and unnecessary work, not to mention stress, for the already challenged swing.

When you see an arrow on your middle maps, will it describe a journey that is about to happen or has already happened? Sticking to either one of these options consistently will preserve the meaning of your rehearsal notes and improve the useability of your future swing bible if the same option is maintained.

TWO TYPES OF TRAFFIC

1. Independent

When a track travels but does not encounter another track, their resulting traffic is known to be independent. Recording independent traffic is made easy by using a continuous arrow.

The Law of Traffic

In the diagram below, when Tracks A and B travel across stage to replace each other, which track will pass downstage?

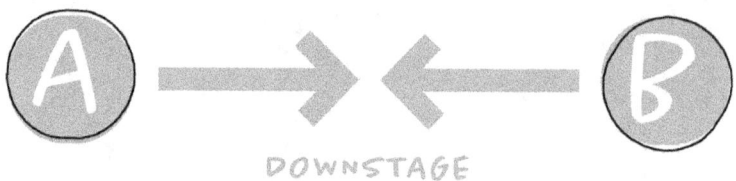

Figure 7.10 Two tracks try to trade places

The Law of Traffic says that:

When two tracks pass, it is custom procedure for the track farthest stage left to pass downstage.

During a creative process, you are likely to hear the phrase 'stage left (SL) crosses downstage (DS) of stage right (SR)' as standard.

If we apply the Law of Traffic to Figure 7.10, Track B should pass DS of Track A.

Figure 7.11 The Law of Traffic

Since the paths of A and B do not intersect, as shown in Figure 7.11, both their journeys can be described as independent and hence continuous arrows can be used for both paths that **will be** taken.

Noticing when a production predominantly obeys the Law of Traffic is one of the most valuable observations a swing can make. By simply remembering SL passes DS of SR, a swing can, in an instant, process the vast majority of traffic in that production.

2. Intersectant

    As the name would suggest, when the traffic of one track intersects with another, traffic is known to be intersectant. The exact point at which the tracks intersect is known as a junction.

TWO TYPES OF ARROW

Just as drivers determine who has the right of way at a junction by reading road signs, we can design our arrows to tell us which track has right of way on stage.

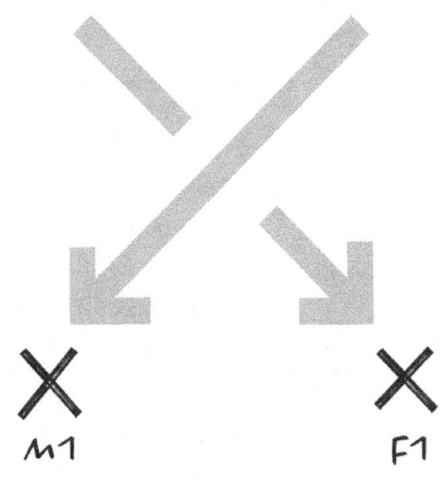

DOWNSTAGE

Figure 7.12 Two tracks at a junction

In Figure 7.12, the continuous arrow has right of way and so M1 passes in front of F1 or we could say that F1 lets M1 cross first.

Since the traffic of M1 is independent (their overall journey is uninterrupted), it is represented by a continuous arrow. The overall journey of F1 is interrupted by M1; it is therefore described as intersectant and is represented by a broken arrow.

This example obeys the Law of Traffic.

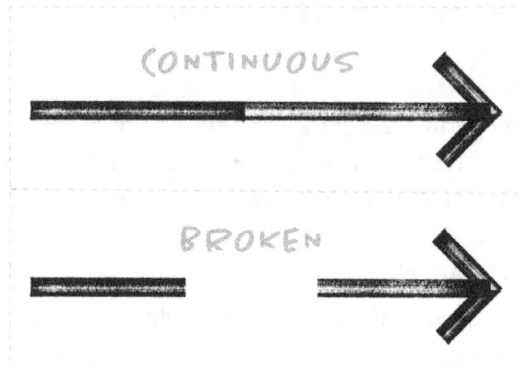

Figure 7.13 Continuous vs. broken arrows

Table 7.2 Definitions of continuous and broken arrows

Definitions of a continuous arrow	Definitions of a broken arrow
Independent traffic	Intersectant traffic
This track crosses first	This track crosses after
This track goes in front	This track goes behind
This track has right of way	This track does not have right of way
This track travels DS of all others	This track travels US of another

Table 7.2 demonstrates the many ways the same arrow can be interpreted to mean the same thing. When taking all this in, remember that you have agreed your arrows will either speak to the future or past events. The full translations of all arrows from a swing map should therefore begin 'this track *will*' or 'this track *has*'.

MULTIPLE TRACKS AT A JUNCTION

What about when more than two tracks cross at the same junction? As a shorthand method, we can try ordering the tracks as they are seen to leave the junction, for example:

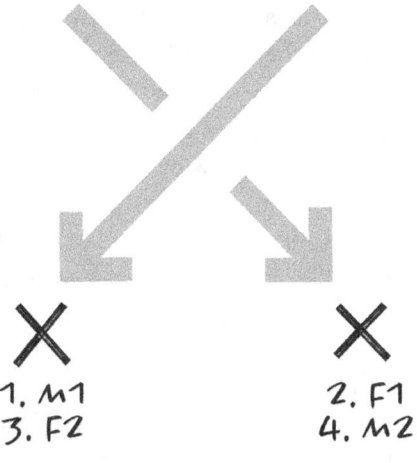

Figure 7.14 Multiple tracks at a junction

In Figure 7.14, the continuous arrow has right of way:

1. M1 crosses first, ahead of F1
2. M2 crosses last
3. F1 passes in front of F2

This example obeys the Law of Traffic.

AFTER STAGE LEFT

Choreographers and ensemble tracks could be easily tempted to make the decision of who has right of way at a junction a matter of flipping a coin.

Figure 7.15 After you

We know, however, that the workload of a swing is radically reduced when a production obeys the Law of Traffic.

In reality, no two paths can truly intersect at a junction simultaneously (unless one track climbs on top of the other). As they are seen to pass, one track will always be in full view of the audience, meaning one track always takes an independent route farther downstage.

Instead of flipping a coin, all creatives and ensemble tracks could help minimise the workload of swings by replacing the phrase 'after you' with the phrase 'after stage left'. By doing so, the traffic in a production will consistently obey the Law of Traffic allowing the swing to remember just one rule for most encounters:

When two tracks pass, it is custom procedure for the track farthest stage left to pass downstage. Abbreviated that is, "SL crosses DS of SR" or in short, "after SL".

MULTIPLE TRACKS AT MULTIPLE JUNCTIONS

Of course, there will always be a time and place for randomised traffic in musical theatre. For example, 20 tracks passing identically – after stage left – in a marketplace would produce a clinical scene. When mass ensemble movement is created to look intentionally random or even frenetic, multiple journeys which both obey and disobey the Law of Traffic happen at different and overlapping times. As a result, a swing is often tasked with making logical sense on paper despite that reality looks like absolute nonsense. There are two mainstream lines of attack they can consider:

A) A collection of middle maps for each track to describe the sequential journeys they take.
B) One very busy middle map representing the staggered journeys of multiple tracks.

Too many middle maps (Option A) will cost a swing the time it takes to chart them. Too much information on one middle map (Option B) risks cramming. Cramming makes your swing bible lighter to carry but harder to read.

To make a considered choice, we can be guided by the SAFE Principles: Option B offers a better representation of the bigger picture and therefore better satisfies the A-Principle.

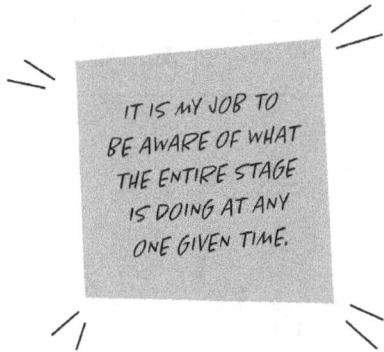

Figure 7.16 Quoted A-Principle

To represent random ensemble movement on one middle map (Option B) without cramming the page, the overall traffic of each track can be broken down into small independent and intersectant journeys. Between each small journey, we find pit stops – places where a track might, among other things, pause, change direction, deliver dialogue, improvise or perform choreography before they commence their next small journey. In list form, the journey of one ensemble track amid random ensemble movement might read as:

1. Start position (×)
2. Independent traffic (arrow)
3. Pit stop (1)
4. Independent traffic (arrow)
5. Pit stop (2)
6. Independent traffic (arrow)
7. End (3)

> PIT STOP: A brief pause taken by a track along the course of a longer journey.

The same journey can be represented pictorially as a timeline of pit stops and arrows:

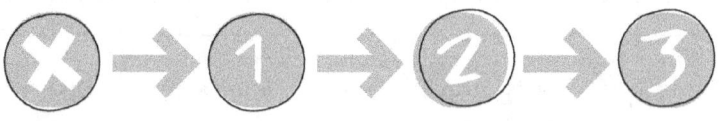

Figure 7.17 Pit stop timeline

The same track journey can be layered with other track journeys on the same map, as seen in the example provided.

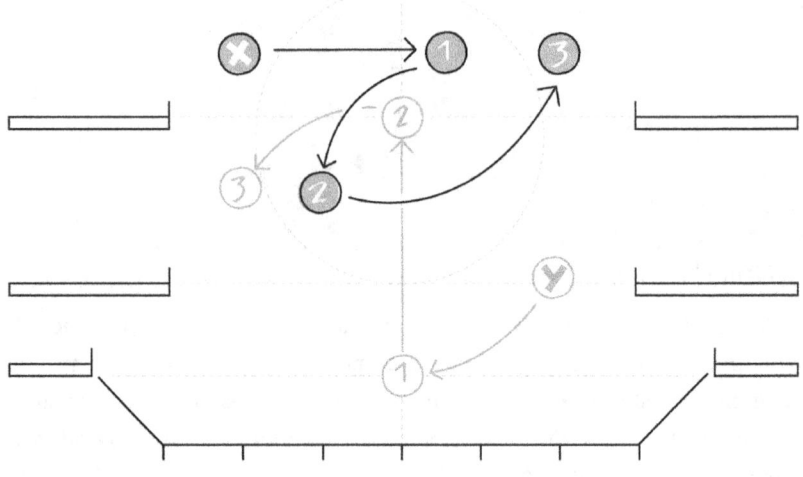

Figure 7.18 Example of traffic map using pit stops

Whenever cramming threatens to reduce the practicality of a map, start a new one. You would not keep stuffing a shopping bag when it is full, so do not stuff your maps!

HOW TO RECORD WHEN

Imagine a script filled with what you say but missing what others say in between. You would know what to say but you would have no indication of when to say it. Put simply, it's a hopeless script. What we come to appreciate is that information is meaningless unless we know when to action it, just as your rehearsal notes would be meaningless unless you record *when* everything happens in the form of cues.

CUE: A time indicator which informs precisely when to take action.

The title of a swing map is one example of a cue, it tells us both what we are looking at and, more specifically, when to expect what is pictured to happen. An equally valid version of your minimum presentation checklist would read as follows:

1. A cue
2. A page number
3. A date
4. A DS mark
5. A centre line
6. A width descriptor

The three types of cue are:

1. Aural – something you hear.
2. Physical – something you feel.
3. Visual – something you see.

SCENE WORK VS. PRODUCTION NUMBERS

Scripts are full of aural cues. By and large, performers will take the previous line spoken by another performer as their cue to speak.

Other aural cues include sound effects, such as a doorbell or a phone ringing, which may be found amid the stage directions in the script. Within stage directions, you might also find examples of physical and visual cues:

(DANIEL *throws the pencil to* FRANCIS, *who barely catches*)
(MATTHEW *crosses to the dining table, pulls out a chair and takes a seat, amused.*
   BLACKOUT.)

The catch of the pencil could be both a physical cue for Francis and a visual cue for another track to act.

The actions of Matthew crossing, sitting and the succeeding blackout are all examples of potential visual cues for other tracks.

Pay attention to any cues that are added by a director to suit their vision for the production. For example, they may choose to underscore a scene with background music. Say a specific lyric becomes a cue to do something, you will want to add it to your script alongside a note describing the corresponding action of the track concerned.

As opposed to using blueprints to record *where* tracks are and *when* they move in a scene, hereafter 'blocking', it is often more practical to record these variables alongside the relevant cues in the script itself.

> BLOCKING: General term given to the movement of tracks on stage not classified as choreography.

At your earliest opportunity, perhaps before the contract starts, you might request or print a copy of the script that is single sided. Rehearsal notes about blocking can then be taken, less the risk of cramming, on the blank page opposite the script.

For musical numbers that identify more as 'sung scene work' as opposed to 'mass choreography', it may even be preferable to record the blocking of tracks alongside the lyrics as they appear in the script too.

Big production numbers, however, require swing maps on which cues will appear as titles or perhaps short sidenotes in available margin space, for example:

- When M1 passes newspaper to M4
- Lights up
- On conductor upbeat

SHORTHAND FOR COUNTS

Aural cues in production numbers tend to exist as counts. They appear frequently on swing maps, but they need to be written as quickly as they are heard. You can miss an awful lot while taking the time to record just one aural cue: the third count in the fourth lot of eight.

The following is a suggested shorthand for recording counts, which we will refer to as 'SAFE shorthand'. It is not guaranteed to serve every swing, but it may help inspire the conception of your own shorthand or confirm that you prefer to write counts as longhand cues. The bottom line is that the only person your shorthand needs to make sense to, is you.

When we count, in the English language, we start with the big stuff. We say five thousand, six hundred and seventy-eight not eight, seventy, six hundred and five thousand. If the latter were true, I would forgive you for mistakenly writing 8,765 instead of 5,678. SAFE shorthand starts with the big stuff too.

The lot

When compositions are written down, it is split up into 'bars' of music. In music theory, the number of musical beats in a bar is known as the time signature. Consecutive bars of music are numbered in ascending order which helps choreographers to pinpoint where they would like a rehearsal pianist to play from.

Musicians split music up into 'bars' of beats whereas performers split music up into 'lots' of counts. In essence, bars and lots serve the same purpose: they divide a big piece of music into smaller chunks. Beats and counts are synonymous with each other too. For a musical number with a time signature of 4/4 (that is 4 beats to a bar), performers will count the music in lots of 8 counts.

> Somewhat confusingly, in the US, you are more likely to hear 'the first *count* of 8' as opposed to 'the first *lot* of 8 counts'.

As a result of the frequency of 4/4 songs in musical theatre, it is indeed a rare occasion that you will hear a dancer count to 9. The following is therefore a likely transcript of a choreographer staging a production number in rehearsal:

1, 2, 3, 4, 5, 6, 7, 8,
1, 2, 3, 4, 5, 6, 7, 8,
1, 2, 3, 4, 5, 6, 7, 8

... and so on. Suppose now the choreographer asks a company to rewind and reset to count 3. Well, you might ask, 'Which count of 3 exactly?'. To know, the choreographer needs to specify which lot of 8 the requested count of 3 belongs to. To help keep track of lots in the rehearsal room, a different transcript is heard far more often:

1, 2, 3, 4, 5, 6, 7, 8,
2, 2, 3, 4, 5, 6, 7, 8,
3, 2, 3, 4, 5, 6, 7, 8

... and so on. Notice the first count of each new lot of 8 has been replaced by the cumulative number of lots that have been counted so far.

> Don't get too cosy, musical numbers come in all sorts of time signatures and may not even stick to the same one for its duration. I have swung on productions where the number of counts in a lot flipped unpredictably from 7 to 4 to 3 to 8 and back to 7 again.

When a swing needs to record a count as a cue to do something, they must first record which lot that count belongs to AKA write the big stuff first.

Used in speech and written in longhand as 'the first lot of eight' or 'the fourth lot of six', SAFE shorthand uses brackets to indicate the lot. For example,

(1) = the first lot
(4) = the fourth lot

SAFE shorthand uses the multiplication symbol (×) to specify the number of counts in each lot whereby:

(1) × 8 = the first lot of eight counts
(4) × 6 = the fourth lot of six counts

The whole count

Smaller than the lot is the whole count, used in speech and written in longhand as 'count three'. Written using SAFE shorthand, whole counts are represented by the corresponding digit. For example,

3 = count three
(1)3 = count three in the first lot

> Notice that (1)3 and (1) × 3 do not translate the same. The first describes the isolated count of three and the second describes the first lot of three counts.

Half or quarter counts

In the UK, the words 'and' and 'a' are used interchangeably to specify half, quarter and eighth counts as in counts '3 and 4', '5 and a 6' or '7 and and a 8'. SAFE shorthand uses the letter 'a' for recording 'a' and the addition symbol '+' for recording 'and'. For example,

3 + 4 = three and four
5 + a 6 = five and a six

Sometimes, swings need to isolate a lone half or quarter count in their notes. An isolated '+' or 'a' becomes less meaningful however if it is not bookended by the whole counts either side. To avoid confusion, SAFE shorthand places one or both of the surrounding whole counts somewhere nearby the relevant half or quarter count. In the examples that follow, the half or quarter count is underlined to highlight them specifically as the intended cue.

3 ± 4 = half count between whole counts 3 and 4
a 6 = quarter count before count 6

Putting it all together, starting with the big stuff and ending with the small stuff, if a cue were 'the half count between 3 and 4 in the 1st lot' it is written using SAFE shorthand as '(1)3±'.

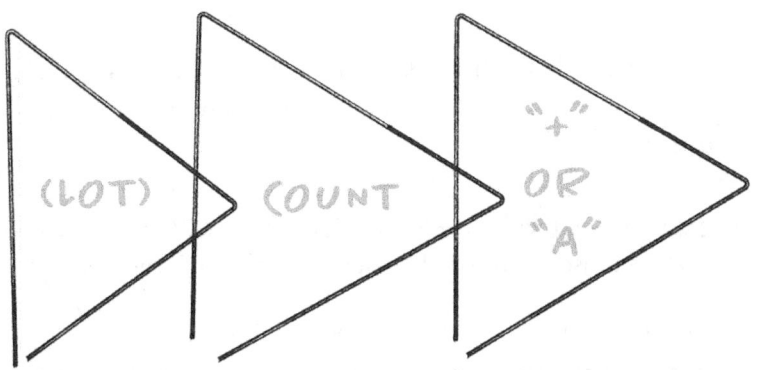

Figure 7.19 SAFE shorthand for counting cues

SHORTHAND FOR DURATION

As well as being able to record when something happens (cues), swings will need to record how long something happens for (duration).

Short duration

When an action takes place within a single lot, SAFE shorthand inserts a dash between the starting and ending counts. For example, when the lot is made up of eight counts, to record that a track walks in slow motion over counts 1 through 4, SAFE shorthand would read as 'slow motion walk for 1–4'.

To specify in which lot eight this happens, the SAFE shorthand for the lot is combined with the shorthand for duration whereby:

Table 7.3 Example of SAFE shorthand for short duration

Longhand	First lot	+	Counts one to four	=	Counts one to four of the first lot
SAFE shorthand	(1)		1–4		(1) 1–4

The SAFE shorthand 'slow motion walk for (1) 1–4' means to walk in slow motion for the first four counts of the first lot.

Long duration

When an action takes place for multiple lots, SAFE shorthand inserts a multiplication symbol between the number of lots and the number of counts per lot. For example, 'Three lots of eight' would become '3×8'.

> Notice that 3×8 and $(3) \times 8$ do not have the same translation. The first describes three lots of eight and the second describes the third lot of eight counts.

To specify when these three lots of eight happen, SAFE shorthand for long duration must be preceded by the starting count whereby:

Table 7.4 Example of SAFE shorthand for long duration

Longhand	Starting the second lot	For two lots of eight	=	Start on the second lot for two lots of eight
SAFE shorthand	(2)	2×8		(2) 2×8

The same applies for any long duration that starts mid lot and carries over into subsequent lots whereby:

Table 7.5 Example of SAFE shorthand for long duration across lots

Longhand	Starting on count 2 of the third lot	...	For two lots of eight	=	Start on count two of the third lot for two lots of eight
SAFE shorthand	(3)2		2 × 8		(3)2, 2 × 8

Note that I have inserted a choice comma between the starting count and the duration for additional clarity. You might do the same or insert words as necessary to meet your needs. For example:

Table 7.6 Personalised example of SAFE shorthand for long duration

Longhand	Starting on count two of the third lot	...	For two lots of eight	=	Start on count two of the third lot for two lots of eight
SAFE shorthand	(3)2		2 × 8		Start (3)2 for 2 × 8

At the end of this chapter, you should be able to:

- ❏ Confidently define Blocking, Coding, Charting/Mapping, Cue, Layer and Pit Stops.
- ❏ Suggest a consistent method that describes how you will code track names.
- ❏ Explain how charting is used to accurately record the position and traffic of tracks.
- ❏ Understand the difference between independent and intersectant traffic and suggest how to represent each using basic notation.
- ❏ State the Law of Traffic and explain how it can be employed to lessen the workload of a swing.
- ❏ Use pit stops to record complex random ensemble movement on swing maps.
- ❏ Name three types of cue.
- ❏ Conceive a preliminary shorthand for recording isolated counts and duration.

8. SPEED OF NOTATION

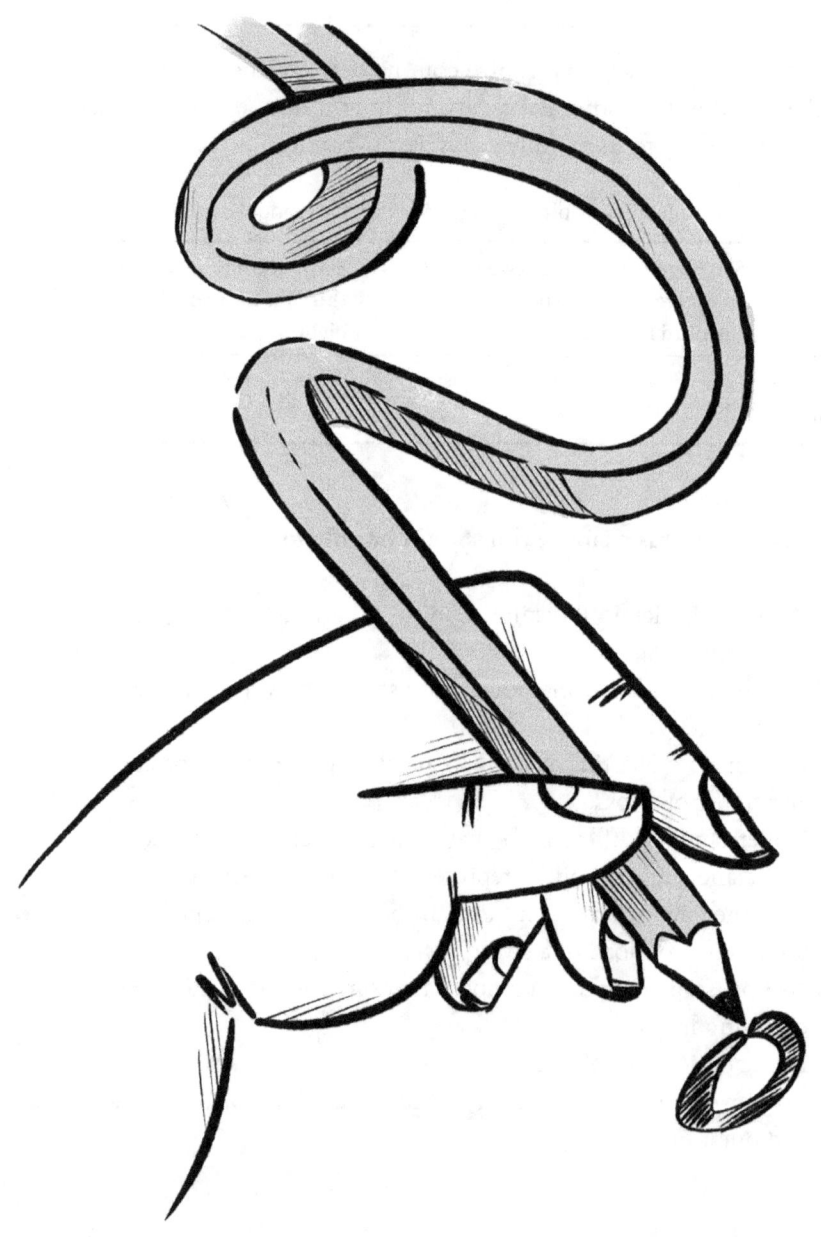

Speed of notation

Eight

A swing ready to absorb new information has their eyes up and their ears open; they have the look of an alert Labrador waiting to be thrown a stick. In contrast, a swing with their eyes down, putting pencil to paper is less likely to see or hear new information as it is given. Despite that you are now prepared with your basics of notation to increase your speed when recording variables, there are some more preference-based techniques we can explore together to help us maintain a more Labrador-like state.

The SAFE Strategy summarises what we have learnt so far as follows:

Swings record the variables by maximising their speed of notation to take rehearsal notes which affords them time to embody the ingredients by getting up and practicing.

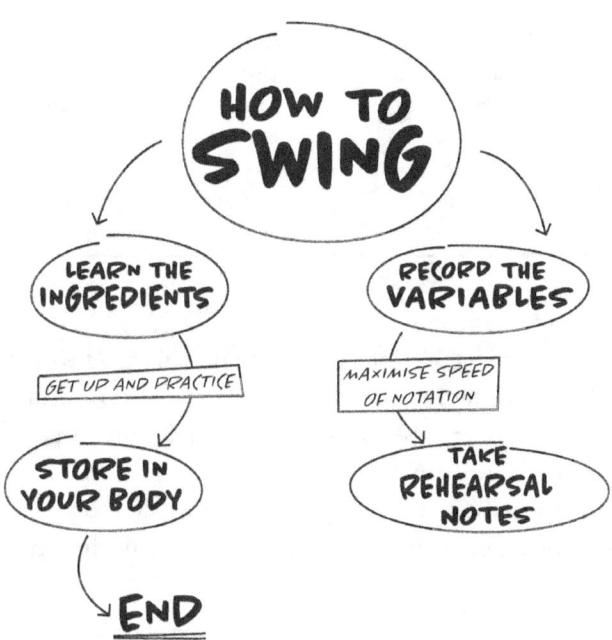

Figure 8.1 The SAFE Strategy: In the rehearsal process

DOI: 10.4324/9781003254300-9

> All this emphasis on speed is likely to cause silly mistakes to be made. Imagine leaving out the letter 'b' in the abbreviation 'tbsp' for tablespoon in cooking. It would be an easy mistake to make but the resultant teaspoon (tsp) measure of sugar would have damaging effects to the sweetness of the cake you bake. When using the following preference-based techniques, be careful not to forego detail or compromise clarity in the name of speed.

COMMON REHEARSAL ROOM ABBREVIATIONS

Each swing will have a unique vocabulary list they use to describe movement; words which they come to record time and time again. Some productions, choreographers and directors use specific words so often that they become endearingly associated with them.

To save time scribbling, you can think about how you would abbreviate the most common terms heard in rehearsal rooms, some of which are listed in the table below:

Table 8.1 Overheard in the rehearsal room

Left	Stage left	Inside	Strike
Right	Stage right	Outside	Cross
Upstage	Upstage left/right	Up	Turn
Downstage	Downstage left/right	Down	Group
Centre	Onstage	High	With
Spike	Offstage	Low	Without
In front	Behind	Forward	Backward
Towards	Between	Opposite	Together

Left and Right

If there were a league table for the most frequently used words in direction and choreography, left and right would surely top it. Among plenty more contexts, they are used to describe which arm to use, in which direction to travel and which wing to enter or exit from.

Almost universally, 'left' and 'right' are abbreviated to a capital 'L' and 'R' respectively. While these two letters prove effective in most contexts, they can lead to some confusion when used to describe wings and stage numbers.

A production with three wings or less can differentiate each using the terms downstage, midstage and upstage. Productions with three or more wings are likely to number them where 'Wing 1' correlates with the wing farthest downstage.

When wings are numbered, it would be easy to doubt whether an abbreviation like 'R1' refers to the extreme downstage right wing or the first stage number on stage right of centre. As a solution and general rule of thumb, I always found it useful to describe wings with a letter first and stage number with a number first so that:

- 'R1' refers to the extreme downstage right wing.
- '1R' refers to the first stage number on stage right of centre.

Onstage and offstage

Where upstage and downstage describe directions up and down of centre, onstage and offstage describe directions in and out of centre. You may find some swings and productions use 'instage' and 'outstage' interchangeably with onstage and offstage.

To use the term 'onstage' in context, you might record 'all tracks start sequence with onstage leg' meaning all tracks start with the leg nearest centre.

Upward and downward arrows

In swing shorthand, upward (↑) and downward (↓) arrows are commonly used to denote high and low, top and bottom, up and down. They can also be used to describe when tracks:

- Are stood or seated.
- Jump over or duck under.
- Pass props above or below.

In short, upward and downward arrows are very versatile indeed. While I am a champion for consistency, so long as the context is clear, swings need not limit the number of ways they use upward and downward arrows to abbreviate their associated meaning.

The symbol: X

Not to be confused with a crosshair, a larger cross symbol or the capitalised letter X can be translated in many ways. For example,

- To strike/exit a prop from stage.
- To cross legs or arms.
- To cross/pass another track.

SPEED CHARTING

To be speedy, swings are encouraged to record 'necessary information' as opposed to 'as much information as possible'. Necessary information, in the context of charting, denotes recording enough information to be able to add maximum detail later. A process known as speed charting is a good example of how swings exercise their ability to only record necessary information.

> SPEED CHARTING: The art of recording enough information about where tracks are positioned so that comprehensive and accurate swing maps can later be derived.

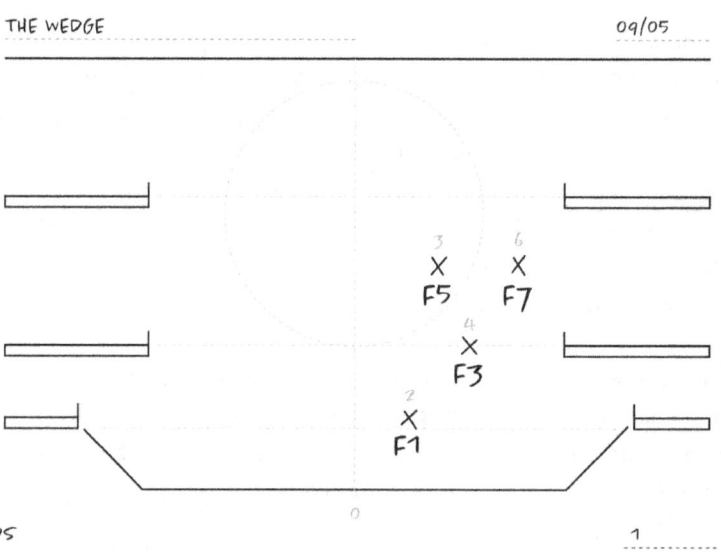

Figure 8.2 Example speed map

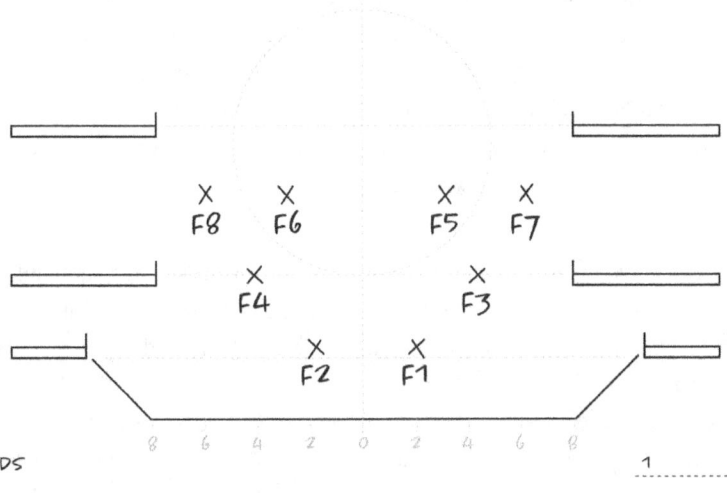

Figure 8.3 Swing map from a speed map

Figure 8.2 shows the speed map recorded in the rehearsal room that has been used to inform the swing map seen in Figure 8.3.

Notice that both maps satisfy the minimum presentation checklist which ensures their meaning can be preserved for as long as possible. The speed map however, exploits a knowledge of the overall pattern to leave out the position of tracks that can be later deduced and added. You can think of speed maps like the roll of a film that gets developed to become the final photographs (swing maps).

In this case the pattern is symmetrical about the centre line which allows the swing to omit all tracks on stage right. If the tracks opposite each other have carried over from a previous swing map (which they often do in big production numbers), swings can trust that they will be able to plug in the missing coded track names on stage right later. In this age of swinging however, you can also use video recordings to complete who belongs to which crosshair on a speed map without distress.

Other formations that can be speed charted include those where any part of the overall pattern is mirrored or repeated, for example rows and columns.

If you have not prepared blank blueprints with a number rule or have no time to draw one afresh on your speed map, Figure 8.2 demonstrates an alternative way to record stage numbers quickly, see how they are recorded above the crosshair of each track.

There is no doubt this technique is accurate, neat and swift but swings should bear in mind how precious leftover space above or below a crosshair can be. Each crosshair will already be labelled with a coded track name and they might want to fill any remaining space with an additional variable such as a cue to move, which direction to face, or which arm to raise. To avoid crowded maps, the default technique for recording stage numbers should always be in relation to a number rule.

> While a swing strives to record accurate information as it is taught, there is no guarantee stage number allocation will remain the same from rehearsal room to stage. In fact, the likelihood of change is extremely high, especially if rehearsing a show in creation. So, if recording stage numbers with impeccable accuracy starts to take away time you could use to practice your template track or relax after work, I recommend recording a quick but good estimate instead.
>
> If rehearsing for a cast change or revival production, stage number allocation is far more reliable because it is information that has been tried and tested under performance conditions. The sooner you can record these accurately, the less work you will have to do later in the swing process.

THE TRACKS SWINGS DO NOT COVER

Male- and female- identifying swings will cover tracks of the respectively identifying sex. First and second cover allocation may then be assigned meaning that the typical covering system for a team of four swings looks as follows:

Table 8.2 First & second swing allocation

	Female tracks				Male tracks			
Swing	F1	F2	F3	F4	M1	M2	M3	M4
Livvy	1st	1st	2nd	2nd				
Samantha	2nd	2nd	1st	1st				
Michael					1st	1st	2nd	2nd
Robert					2nd	2nd	1st	1st

Table 8.2 shows that there are some ensemble tracks Livvy, Samantha, Michael, and Robert do not cover. For example, Livvy does not cover M2 and Michael does not cover F4.

The notion of recording minimum data when speed mapping could encourage a swing to omit information about the tracks they do not cover as seen by the female swing who has left out information about male tracks in the following example:

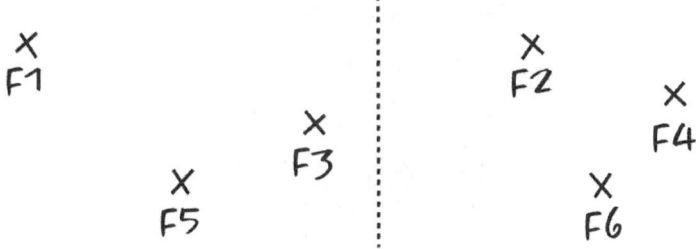

Figure 8.4 Swing map with isolated female tracks

There is very little sense to be made from the resulting pattern which makes the overall formation difficult to process. Now, let us look at the complete picture which charts the male tracks:

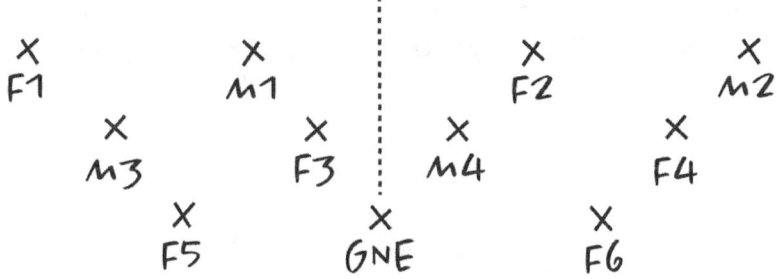

Figure 8.5 Combined swing map with male & female tracks

Without question the pattern is clearer and there is more than one pattern to observe:

1. It is symmetrical.
2. There are three clear rows.
3. Male and female tracks alternate along each row.
4. Offstage tracks form two diagonal lines.
5. Onstage tracks form a V-shape.

Appreciating pattern is a vital swing skill that improves spatial awareness since swings are more likely to position themselves accurately if they understand how they relate to other tracks in a formation. When swings cannot readily access their swing maps, they rely on their knowledge of pattern to inform where they should be in moments of sudden uncertainty.

Figure 8.6 A-Principle

When male and female tracks start to move, it becomes doubly important to chart the traffic of the tracks you do not cover. It is easy to imagine how failure to appreciate the way male tracks move around female tracks in Figure 8.5 would risk collision.

Figure 8.7 Quoted S-Principle

When it comes to how much you need to record about the tracks you do not cover, inclusive of principal roles too, it is the same rule we have seen before: **Record where and when not what.**

You do not need to learn *what* they do but to uphold the SAFE Principles of awareness and safety, you do need to record *where* they are and *when* they move.

The only time a swing need not worry about recording the whereabouts of the tracks they do not cover is when male, female and principal tracks do not interact in any capacity. It is a luxurious position for swings to find themselves in because it is indeed rare.

To go the extra swing mile, if you spot an ensemble track of the opposite sex doing something integral, you might want to write down *what* that track is doing. In a cut-show scenario, it could well be appreciated that you could step in for that particular moment since without it, the show would not be possible.

MIDDLE CHARTING

There are three stages to any given journey of a track: beginning (stationary), middle (moving) and end (stationary). In the following examples of each map, crosshairs represent stationary positions and arrowheads arrive accurately at resultant stationary positions.

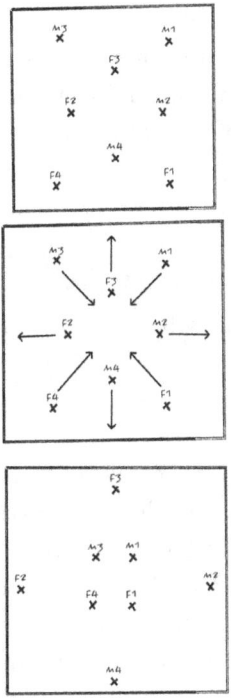

Figure 8.8 A beginning map, a middle map and an end map

We can deduce all three stages of a journey from the middle map; it shows the pathways of each track as well as their beginning and ending positions.

Novice swings are sometimes reluctant to layer information about traffic on top of their accurate beginning map because they took such care to draw it in the first place. Confident swings save time by prioritising accurate middle maps in the rehearsal room because they know they can retrieve the relative beginning and end maps later. This shorthand technique is known as middle charting.

> MIDDLE CHARTING: To solely chart the moving map of a journey to increase speed of notation.

Please note, successful middle charting is reliant on the meticulous placement of crosshairs and/or arrowheads. If you are unable to recover accurate stage numbers of both beginning and ending positions from your middle maps, middle charting is not advised.

More chaotic traffic is harder to notate at speed but should not steal time from a swing wanting to get up and practice the ingredients. If multiple journeys are causing you to spend unwanted time writing, it might be wise to add that section of traffic to your 'I don't know' list and simply worry about it later.

> You may be starting to picture swings in a constant rush but a room full of swings with an effective shorthand have all the time they need, to record only what they need, and very little in excess.

DIRECTION VS. TRAFFIC

The terms *direction* and *traffic* are easily confused. When a performer asks, 'What direction do I travel in?' they in fact ask, 'What traffic do I take?' Though the word can be used interchangeably in this context, it is better for swings to understand direction and traffic as two separate entities. You might want to eliminate the word 'direction' altogether and instead adopt the term 'directional front' or simply 'front'.

> DIRECTION/DIRECTIONAL FRONT: An instruction to describe the angle something is facing or a track calls their 'front'.

When blocking or choreography is set facing different angles for visual effect, directional front is a variable that needs to be recorded. Often swings will use the margin space of the corresponding swing map to record descriptive notes about directional front.

As a quick and clear alternative to writing longhand descriptive notes, swings can use layers to record instructions about directional front. Just as we can layer traffic onto a stationary map, we can also layer directional front in one of two ways:

1. If a directional rule can be applied, the map can be divided pictorially and labelled using arrows. Note that Figure 8.9 assumes the directional rule does not apply to the principal role coded by 'GNE'.

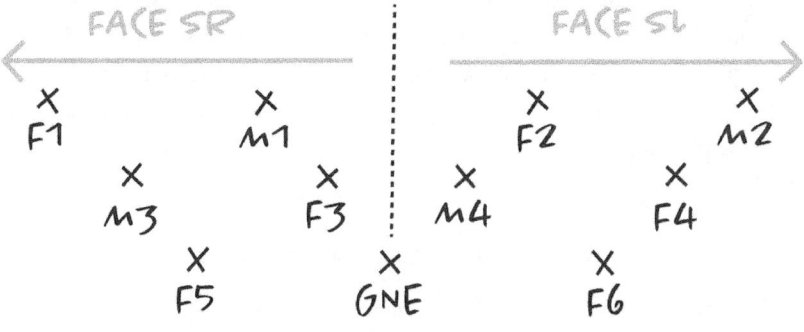

Figure 8.9 Swing map layered with directional rule

You might scribble 'all tracks face away from centre' or 'face partner'. In either scenario, would you consider directional front to be a variable or an ingredient? While tracks can technically be said to face a different directional front, one universal rule can be applied to all tracks. Universal instruction is an ingredient, something to be embodied and not recorded. Still, plenty of swings choose to record a universal directional rule just in case they forget it.

2. If directional front is assigned in a more sporadic fashion, each cross hair might be labelled with a directional arrow:

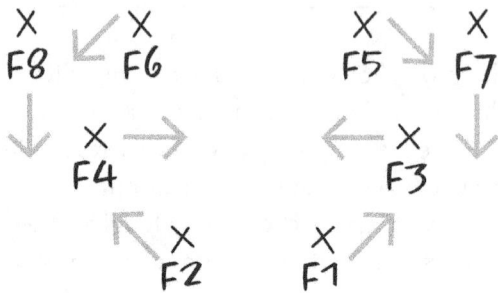

Figure 8.10 Labelling crosshairs with directional arrows

> To chart a map for the specific purpose of recording directional front, you might like to plot hollow circles instead of crosshairs and attach a directional cone or arrow to each. Your coded names would live inside each circle. If, however, the purpose of the swing map is also to depict accurate position, the use of crosshairs must be reinstated because only a point of intersection can represent exact position.

Until now, arrows have been used consistently to describe one of the following:

a) Traffic that will happen.
b) Traffic that has happened.

So as not to cause confusion or waste any previous effort to make sure your arrows have consistent meaning, swings must consider how they will tell the difference between an arrow that describes traffic and an arrow that describes directional front.

Personally, I never found a perfect solution, but it was also rare that I needed to record both on the same swing map. As such, context played a large part in being able to tell whether my arrows described traffic or directional front.

In the unusual position that you need to describe traffic and directional front on the same map, reserve your arrows for traffic and jot down what you need know about directional front somewhere close by.

RECORDING CANON

If you have ever sung a song 'in a round', you will have performed in a form of canon. In the UK, the most relatable example of this tends to be a song from childhood, Frère Jacques, in which two or more groups sing the same song but each group starts singing slightly after one another.

> CANON: When the same ingredients are performed at staggered times causing a ripple effect.

Dancing in a round is better known as dancing in canon and it is often used to great visual effect in musical numbers. Each group performs the same choreographic sequence but their cue to start is increasingly delayed so that the first group dances, followed by a second, followed by a third and so on. A canon may complete over time, meaning the group of tracks that starts last also finishes last, or on a unison count, causing the group that starts last to finish mid sequence.

When canon is used, and especially when the interval between groups is irregular, swings use their shorthand for counts to quickly record when each group starts the sequence. Using the SAFE shorthand we learnt in Chapter 7, Table 8.3 shows how you might record the starting counts of a canon made up of three groups:

Table 8.3 Shorthand cues per canon group

Group	Cue to start
1	(1)1
2	(1)5
3	(2)1

Since pictures can say a 1,000 words, the same information can be recorded quickly as a layer on swing maps too. This is particularly appropriate when canon is allocated according to where tracks are positioned as demonstrated by Figure 8.11:

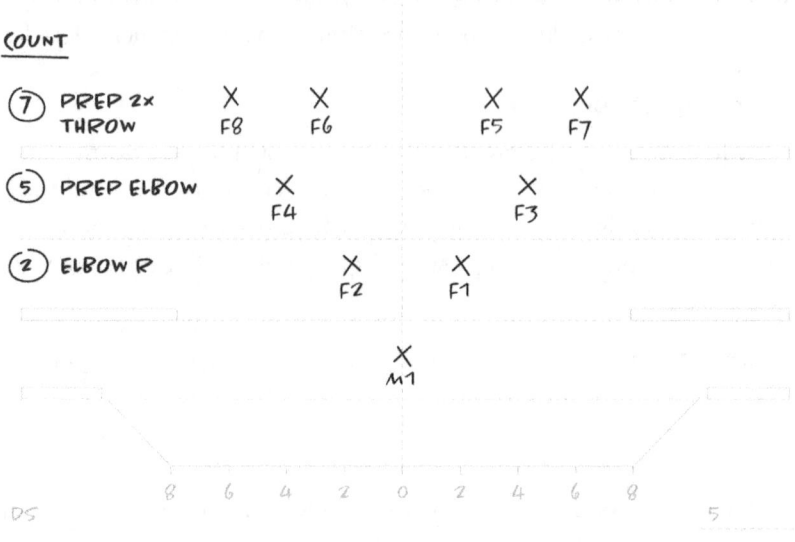

Figure 8.11 Swing map layered with canon

By recording canon as a pictorial layer, it is easier to notice the resultant visual effect such that, in the example of Figure 8.11, groups join in from the front to the back. In time, you might hope to remember this canon through the action of notating it pictorially in the first place. You might employ the same tactic for any other kind of variable that is assigned with an overall visual effect in mind.

In the canons so far described, *when* each group starts the choreography has been different but *what* choreography each group starts with has been the same. In a different kind of canon, known informally as a 'build-up', each track joins in at different times and with different choreography.

Imagine an empty dancefloor at a celebration which is first filled by a single couple. Next a group of friends decide they would like to dance too and before long the dancefloor is filled with various collections of people dancing. When this scene, or similar, is replicated in a musical, swings record when each group joins the dancefloor as a variable and learn any necessary ingredients as separate entities.

Now imagine the same empty dancefloor but fill it with someone performing a line dance. More and more people catch on to the choreography and join in so that the dancefloor fills with people doing the same choreography in unison. For want of a modern-day reference, this version of a build-up is a bit like a flash mob. To record this scene, any of the following can be recorded to remember at what point each group joins the fixed choreographic sequence:

A) A count
B) A lyric
C) A recognisable step from the line dance

As an example of both options A and C, take a look back at Figure 8.11 and realise its very fitting title as a specific type of canon: The Build-Up.

SHORTHAND FOR LYRICS

Not all performers enjoy counting music and not all creatives work to counts. No matter, every performer will encounter times when it is impractical to record counts and easier to record lyrics.

Longhand lyrical cues often appear as titles of swing maps. Much like counting cues though, swings often need to break lyrics down so that they reflect a snippet of time. This is made easy when a lyric has one syllable such as 'love', but what if a track performs an action on just part of a word; for example, they jump on the 'ter' of 'afternoon'?

There are several ways to highlight a particular syllable as a cue including but not limited to:

- Underlining: af ter noon
- Use of capitals: af TER noon
- Use of brackets: af (ter) noon

Beats or counts between lyrics should be treated as honorary syllables so that if you needed to highlight the beat between the lyrics 'love' and 'afternoon' as a cue, you could record:

- love beat afternoon
- love BEAT afternoon
- love (beat) afternoon

CONSISTENCY OF SHORTHAND

Your shorthand will consist of any number of abbreviations and charting methods, not limited to those we have so far explored. Only increased experience will teach you which techniques will be of greatest benefit to your speed of notation. That said, a novice with a consistent shorthand is far quicker at recording variables than an inconsistent veteran. So, even if you are just starting out, no moment is too soon to begin making choices about your consistent shorthand. You can always adapt it to suit any preferences you discover as you swing along.

> **At the end of this chapter, you should be able to:**
>
> ❏ Practice abbreviating the most commonly heard vocabulary in a rehearsal room of a musical.
> ❏ Confidently define Canon, Direction, Middle Charting and Speed Charting.
> ❏ Use speed charting and middle charting to record position and traffic quickly and accurately.
> ❏ Comment on the importance of charting tracks swings do not cover on swing maps.
> ❏ Layer swing maps with information about variables such as directional front and canon.
> ❏ Record lyrics as shorthand cues.

9. INFORMATION OVERLOAD

Information overload

Nine

Sometimes the rehearsal room moves so fast that despite our best efforts to scribble our shorthand, we just cannot keep up!

Have you ever spent too much time worrying about what you have missed that you continue to miss new information? It happens to me whenever I watch a fast-paced spy movie, fortunately the buttons stop, rewind and play on my remote control always come to my rescue.

When swings obsess over something they might have missed, they ignore what is happening in the present and subsequently miss even more information. I call it, the 'Fear Of Missing Information' effect, or for a fun acronym 'FOMI'.

Figure 9.1 The FOMI effect.

When you cannot keep up and FOMI starts to take hold, it is a good idea to stop what you are doing and prioritise.

HOW TO LIMIT PRIORITIES

Of prioritising Jim Collins, author of From Good to Great, explains that:

'if you have more than three priorities, you have no priorities'.

Imagine you are a swing trying to juggle five "priorities" at once:

1. Where are tracks positioned?
2. What is the choreography?
3. Who crosses downstage of who to change formation?
4. Who passes what prop to who?
5. When does each prop get passed?

How does managing all of that information at once make you feel? Of course, you may rise to the challenge but in case it all gets the better of you, first try following the advice of Jim Collins and reduce your number of priorities to just two.

First priority of a swing

Figure 9.2 F-Principle

You will remember from Chapter 6 – *How to Record the Variables* – that the first priority of swings in rehearsal is to serve function. When feeling overwhelmed, swings identify what they need to learn most urgently to enable them to step in at a moment's notice. Might it be learning *what* tracks are doing or *where* tracks are going? Over the initial rehearsal weeks, a priority to serve function will mostly guide swings to practice the ingredients of their template track.

Second priority of a swing

The second priority of swings is to remember what they pushed aside to serve function as their first priority. Suppose, unusually, that a swing needed to prioritise *where* tracks were for a time, they will need to remember that they in turn postponed learning some ingredients say, a choreographic combination. Smart swings expect to postpone more information than they can take a mental note of and so choose to keep a written log instead.

I love the saying 'A place for everything and everything in its place' because sticking to it has brought me invaluable peace over the years. The best place to log things you postpone learning, or recording, is on your 'I don't know' list. Remember that designated space we set aside at the back of your notebook in Chapter 4? Prepare to use it to keep FOMI at bay.

It is important that you manage your 'I don't know' list by deleting items from it as soon as they are learnt because organisation breeds composure. Also, before swinging on for a track, I would scan my 'I don't know' list to make doubly sure that there were no holes in my knowledge that could catch me off guard. Naturally, I wouldn't always have the time to be so diligent but there were certainly some occasions when I was glad that I had made the time.

When a rehearsal room starts to run away from a swing, they reduce their priorities to two:

1. Focus on that which serves function.
2. Keep an up-to-date 'I don't know' list.

> Be pro-active about reducing the number of items listed on your 'I don't know' list. After all, to make a list and then let your unknowns gather dust is as good as forgetting the information you did not learn in the first place.

VIDEO RECORDING

These days, if you miss the live show in rehearsal or feel overwhelmed by it, you can literally watch it on playback later. Cameras on smart phones and tablets offer an incredible way of recording a lot of information quickly and are certainly a perk of 21st century swinging.

It is always worth trying to capture rehearsal videos from multiple angles, so that you can fill in any blind spots from one recording by referencing another. As a swing, there are additional advantages to recording rehearsals from 'behind', that is from upstage of the action or from a performer's perspective:

- It is easier to follow along with a video that matches the performer's point of view.
- Swings are able to better imagine themselves amongst the surrounding tracks.

Conversely, when you replay a video that has been recorded from the audience's perspective, everything appears as a mirror image, which can be very confusing. If you survived teaching, or learning, dance using video conferencing during the COVID pandemic, you will know exactly the kind of struggle I am referring to. One day I dream of the technology that allows swings to record a rehearsal and then, using 3D imaging, replay the footage in virtual reality. For now though, 2D playback from the back of a rehearsal room is your best offer.

> A team of swings might like to develop a system whereby one swing records a video from downstage of the action while another records from an upstage position. Both videos should subsequently be shared with the entire team.

But, as with anything, if something seems too good to be true, it probably is. In the context of filming rehearsals, you may come up against some common hurdles.

Video recording is not permitted in all rehearsal rooms

The child protection system limits filming on productions that feature young performers. To overcome this obstacle, a dance captain or other allocated person will likely be given sole permission to film. Commonly, these videos can be watched on site, on a company owned device or via a secure link. To find out how you can watch protected videos, you should seek the instruction of a line manager such as your company manager, resident director or dance captain.

While safeguarding could prohibit you from filming rehearsals, there may be times when you decide not to film out of courtesy for your fellow cast. Rehearsals are a vulnerable time for performers as they learn their track and experiment with different performance choices. Before you film, I highly recommend asking for advance permission from the relative onstage cast. This is particularly encouraged if you are working with celebrity or high-profile performers, but it would only be polite to extend your courtesy to the entire cast over time. It would be easy to brand a performer 'difficult' for asking a swing not to film but, please remember it is more likely that they are asking for a safe space to make mistakes and ultimately, do their job too.

Lastly, when teams of swings, stage management and resident creatives all want to film rehearsals, a ruling may be put in place to limit the number of persons allowed to film at any one given time. I remember a time when a wall of iPads lined up at the front of a rehearsal room I was working in. The image was so intimidating that, moving forward, only the dance captain was given permission to film and the resultant videos were forwarded to the swings on request.

Videos are never 100% accurate

Of the videos I have taken over the years, few will have been an accurate depiction of what was staged at the time. Performers are not one take wonders; they are human, and humans make mistakes.

You also cannot rely on performers to approach you after filming to say, 'by the way, don't rely on that video because I messed up'. Though, if you are an ensemble performer reading this book, your swing team would be incredibly grateful if you did.

Swings should absolutely embrace the use of video recording to get a rough idea of what was staged but they should never assume what they see is accurate. For the most accurate information, always try to hear everything you can first hand and seek answers to your questions from the people who know best later, such as the onstage performer concerned, your resident director or dance captain.

Videos cannot stay up-to-date

As soon as a production opens to an audience swings rarely get the opportunity to record. Your most up-to-date video footage will therefore be of a run-through in the rehearsal studio or a dress rehearsal.

Videos of studio run-throughs are not reliable because they do not account for changes that happen during the technical rehearsal process. Many of these changes will be made to look after the safety of the cast on stage, meaning information you take from an expired studio run-through could have dangerous repercussions.

> TECHNICAL REHEARSAL: The process of rehearsing a production into the performance space from a design perspective. Technical departments such as costume, wigs, stage management, sound, lighting and automation will rehearse and learn their show around what has been created in the rehearsal room.
>
> DRESS REHEARSAL: A run-through of the production in the performance space with all technical and design elements in play. The first dress rehearsal sits between the end of technical rehearsal and the first performance.

If a swing is able to film a dress rehearsal, they will benefit from having a reference that incorporates changes made during the technical rehearsal process but even that video is not fully reliable as a long-term reference. Productions continue to evolve over time, but change is especially common during the initial playing weeks as people and things settle in.

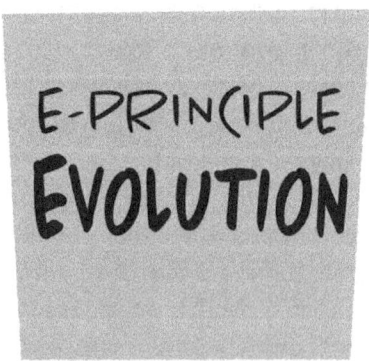

Figure 9.3 E-Principle

In addition to keeping reference videos and making a show bible then, the most thorough swings conduct show watches on a regular basis and every so often, check in with the ensemble cast to find out if anything has changed in recent times. They especially seek to learn smaller changes that happen for practical reasons which might sound like, 'I go downstage now' or, 'Instead, I give my prop directly to stage management when I exit'.

Videos are time consuming

Changes to show set-ups can happen in the blink of an eye. When swings are given minimal notice, it is important that they can do their pre-performance checks quickly. Those working from video can often underestimate the time it takes to find the snippet of a video they need from a library of many. Whereas swings working from a well-presented swing bible can be far more time-efficient when needing to check a specific moment in a show. Chapter 10 – *Ready. Set. Swing bible.* – will begin to explore various presentation methods which seek to increase your speed of information extraction from your swing bible and make you the quickest swing when short of time.

Videos increase total workload

Now you really think I have gone mad – how on earth does filming a rehearsal create more work for swings than charting an entire set of swing maps? As hard as it may be to believe me, in the long run, it does.

There are three separate stages to recording variables in a swing bible:

Step 1: Get them down.
Step 2: Scale them down.
Step 3: Write them up.

It is a process that involves revisiting the same information and deciding if you can remember it or whether it should remain recorded. Along the way, you will also debate the clearest way to present whatever you decide needs to remain recorded. Such frequency of opportunity to assess information can assist your retention of it. I could often recall finer details about a track by mentally retracing the steps I took from first recording a specific variable in the rehearsal room to presenting it in a swing bible. Of course, we make a swing bible expecting to need it, but in an uncanny twist of fate, you may find the practical exercise of making one in fact helps you to swing without.

By comparison, swings who rely on video reference material alone will have spent less time studying the material and hence remain heavily dependent on videos for longer.

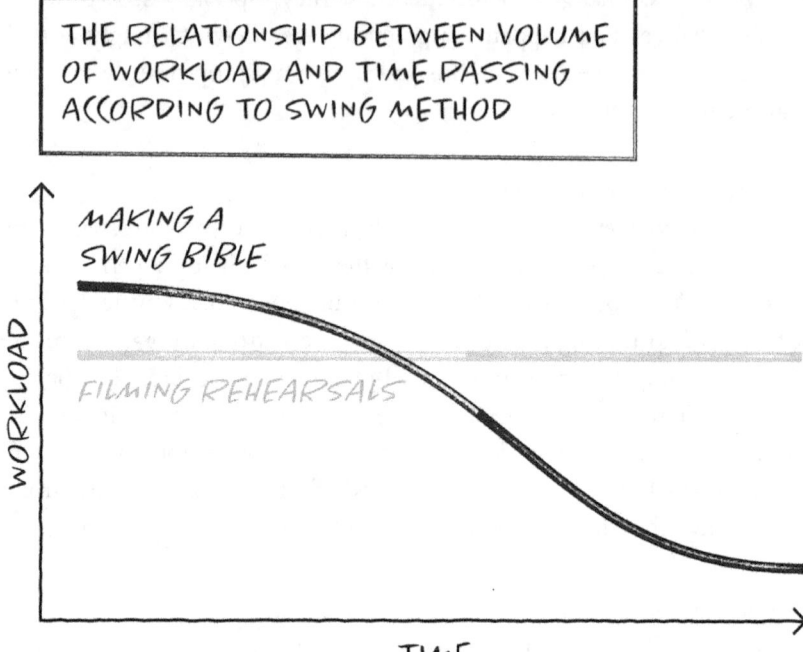

Figure 9.4 Workload: swing bible vs. video recording

Access to videos is not always possible and so any dependency on them will always carry a degree of anxiety. Many stage managers, for reasons that include child performer protection and professionalism, do not permit cast or crew to bring mobile phones to the immediate backstage areas. So, if you think you can swing by having a phone full of videos in the wings, think again.

Swing bibles however have an all-access pass to backstage areas, which alleviates any fear that a swing cannot always be near any last-minute information they might need.

TEAMWORK

It may be considered cliché in some circles but in swing circles we like to remind ourselves that the word 'team' is an acronym for:

T ogether
E everyone

A chieves
M ore

Teamwork does not just extend to your immediate swing team, it can and should extend across the entire cast. Unfortunately, it is common for swings to feel nervous about asking the performers they cover for help. It is an uneasiness that most likely stems from an underlying belief that they are somehow inferior to ensemble cast. It is important for all swings, understudies and onstage cast to understand that swings and understudies can ask an onstage performer they cover for specific information about their track.

If you are an ensemble performer reading this, an effort to check in your swing team, in case they want to ask you anything about your track, is worth its weight in gold.

Swings will need to trust their own good judgement as to the accuracy of the information they receive from onstage cast and, should things not add up, they must remember it is not their responsibility to correct what they hear. Instead, they absorb helpful information and privately disregard anything to the contrary or, if necessary, pass on any unresolved questions to the resident creative team.

Pay attention to the performers that provide more accurate detail than others. Perhaps in overwhelming situations you do not need to focus on their tracks because you know you can seek reliable and useful information from them later.

> The prevailing advice here is to never be afraid to ask. Often, we think that asking questions demonstrates weakness. We think it indicates to others that we are 'out of our depth' or that we have not done a thorough job. It is in fact the opposite, asking questions demonstrates you to be doing a thorough job and I have far more trust in the swings that ask than the swings that do not.

Divide and conquer

The benefit of larger swing teams in overwhelming rehearsal rooms is that they might arrange, for a short time, to focus on one or two tracks each before sharing information learnt with each other later. Most will do so according to their cover allocation so that each swing focuses solely on their first cover tracks. It does however rely on trusting your fellow swings to return the same quality of detail that you intend to give them.

Tempting as it may be to continue in this way, if you narrow your focus to your first cover tracks for too long, you would in fact be engaging in a One-Track-At-A-Time Strategy. To avoid this trap, simply check in with what the bigger picture looks like every so often during the rehearsal and trust it will be clear when you can resume learning a little bit of all tracks simultaneously again. Usually, the switch back to SAFE swinging happens as the rehearsal room slows down and any overwhelming feeling that made you decide to divide and conquer in the first place starts to subside.

Swinging is an extremely individual skill so try not to feel disheartened if the option to divide and conquer is not compatible with the rest of your swing team. That said, it is a healthy habit to talk to your fellow swings, exchange learning styles and debrief rehearsal sessions. You might discover other ways you could work together to ease your individual workload. Indeed, the longer a team of swings work together, the more effective they become as they start to compliment and support their individual learning styles.

MANAGE YOUR EXPECTATIONS

Your own expectations are your biggest threat when you feel bombarded with information. Make sure they are realistic and avoid beating yourself up if what constitutes as 'realistic' means not knowing everything you wish you could. Swinging is a marathon and not a sprint so, above all, be kind to yourself and just do your best.

Figure 9.5 offers a flowchart that might come in handy in times of need. It uses a question we discovered in Chapter 2 – *How to Think Like a Swing* – to help point you in the direction of best serving function. That question was, 'What can I do to help?'

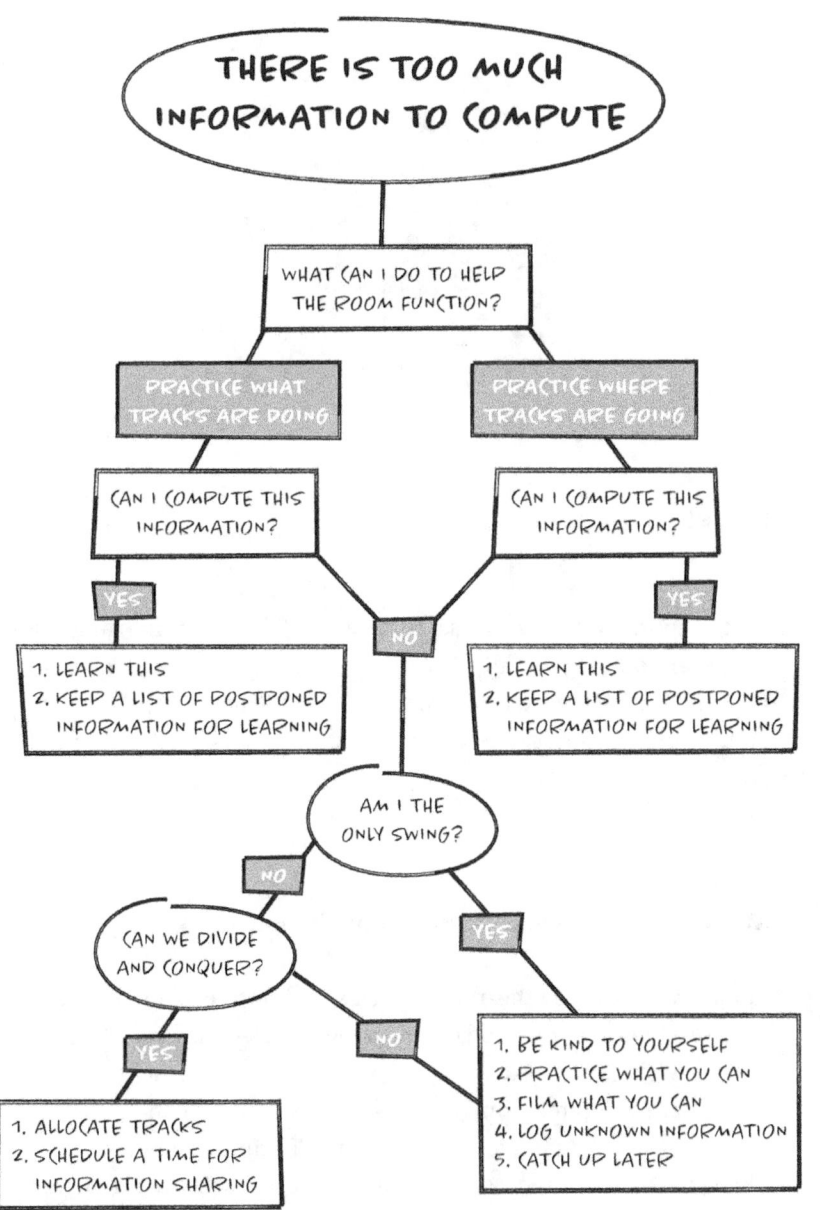

Figure 9.5 Flowchart for runaway rehearsal rooms

Figure 9.6 Quoted F-Principle

It is important to recognise that serving function in runaway rehearsal rooms generally involves getting up and practicing so that you can step in with immediate effect if necessary. It is why Figure 9.5 says to '*practice* where tracks are going' and not '*record* where they are'.

At the end of this chapter, you should be able to:

❑ Manage stressful rehearsal scenarios by limiting your priorities to serving function and keeping a log of postponed information for learning.
❑ Embrace video recording to assist your swing process.
❑ Confidently define Dress Rehearsal and Technical Rehearsal.
❑ Suggest reasons why swings must learn to swing without the use of video recording.
❑ Work as a team of swings to manage overwhelming rehearsal rooms.
❑ Seek the help of onstage cast with confidence.
❑ Imagine what you would do if you were feeling overwhelmed by a fast-paced rehearsal room.

10. READY, SET, SWING BIBLE

Ready. Set. Swing bible.
Ten

When we talk of separating what a swing needs to learn into ingredients and variables, we understand that ingredients are remembered whereas variables are recorded. Swings record every and any variable they can in the rehearsal room, most of which will be collated and stored in a swing bible.

Fortunately, good habits, like satisfying a minimum presentation checklist, ensure that a swing's rehearsal notes make sense to them for a really long time. Ok, so why not use your mountain of rehearsal notes as a swing bible? After all, everything you need to know can be found … somewhere?

To be able to perform at a moment's notice, being a swing requires more than just a comprehensive database of variables. They must be able to extract information from their database or swing bible as quickly as possible.

As a result, between taking rehearsal notes and making a swing bible, there comes a dynamic shift in our approach to recording variables. This is highlighted excellently by the SAFE Strategy which summarises:

> *Swings maximise their speed of notation to take rehearsal notes and then maximise their speed of extraction to make a swing bible.*

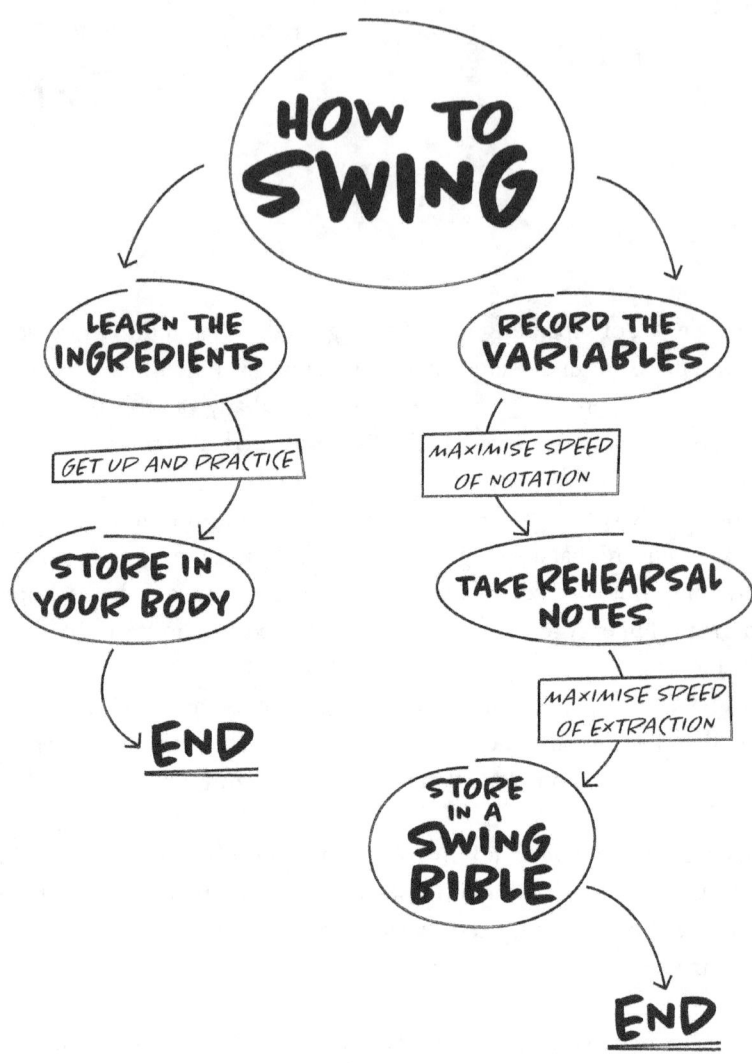

Figure 10.1 The SAFE Strategy: How to make a swing bible

The steps involved in maximising your speed of extraction will consist of tidying, ordering and optimising your rehearsal notes. Your subsequent swing bible will be just like a clutter-free hard drive on a laptop; folders of sacred information stored inside yet more folders and organised expertly so that one can find a specific file at the drop of a hat.

TIDYING A SWING BIBLE

Not everything you find in your rehearsal notes needs to graduate into your swing bible. Redundant notes are those a swing transfers to their swing bible but finds they never revisit. They slow swings down on two accounts:

1. Wasted time presenting them in neat.
2. Wasted time sifting passed them in a swing bible to get to needed information.

> I prefer to use the term redundant notes over superfluous notes. Superfluous suggests they were never worth recording when in fact, you may only come to remember something because you took the time to write it down in the first place.

To avoid transferring redundant notes to a swing bible, swings ask themselves the question, 'Will I remember this information?' If the answer is yes, the information pertains to ingredients and can be disregarded from a swing bible. If the answer is no, the information pertains to variables and must be included in a swing bible. Formally, this tidying process will hereafter be known as 'screening'.

Figure 10.2 Screening notes for a swing bible

> SCREENING: The process of filtering rehearsal notes to disregard ingredients and transfer variables only to a swing bible.

A 2017 survey asked over 100 swings to reflect on the effectiveness of their swing bibles and found that prose notes describing choreography, an ingredient, were the most redundant notes of all. I wonder how many extra hours of sleep those swings could have enjoyed, if they had screened their rehearsal notes more effectively before transferring redundant information to their swing bible.

After screening, a more concise definition of the term swing bible would be as follows:

> SWING BIBLE: The collective term given to documentation used by swings to assist the retention of variables.

ORDERING A SWING BIBLE

Each swing map represents a moment in a show. Swings order their swing bibles chronologically to create a sort of a flip book so that as you flick through the pages, the entire show plays out from a bird's eye view, swing map to swing map, moment to moment. To find information about a specific track, it makes for a very efficient two-step process:

1. Flick to the appropriate moment in the show.
2. Scan for information about a specific track.

If only compiling a swing bible were as simple as putting screened rehearsal notes about variables in order.

OPTIMISING A SWING BIBLE

Imagine I make a shopping list that looks like a stream of consciousness. It is written in my very organised notepad which even has its own section dedicated to shopping lists, ordered according to date. Sure

```
SHOPPING LIST

- BREAD
- MILK
- EGGS
- PASTA
- BANANAS
- STRAWBERRIES
- TOMATOES
- POTATOES
- GARLIC
- LIME
- SOY SAUCE
- JAM
- BUTTER
- SNACKS!!
```

Figure 10.3 A shopping list

enough, I arrive at the supermarket and I am quick to locate the exact list I need. Standing in the vegetable aisle though, I find myself wasting time scanning my list specifically for vegetables. It is at this point that I think, 'Could I have presented this information differently to maximise my speed of extraction?'

The next time I go to the supermarket I have enough time to re-write my list and group items according to aisle number. I cut my time shopping in half.

Another time, I use a highlighter to colour code my unordered list so that I can easily spot the vegetables (newly highlighted in blue) out of the crowd. Again, I save time at the supermarket and for the second time I have a much calmer experience.

Why is this all relevant? Screening and ordering your rehearsal notes are just the tip of the iceberg when it comes to putting your swing bible together. You must consider if there is a better way to present your variables so that you can optimise your speed of information extraction.

A CHOICE OF PERSPECTIVE

The most frequent reason swings revisit swing maps in their swing bible is to check the position of a particular track. Options A and B in Figure 10.4 represent the same formation, but which swing map would help you to step in for Track M2 the quickest?

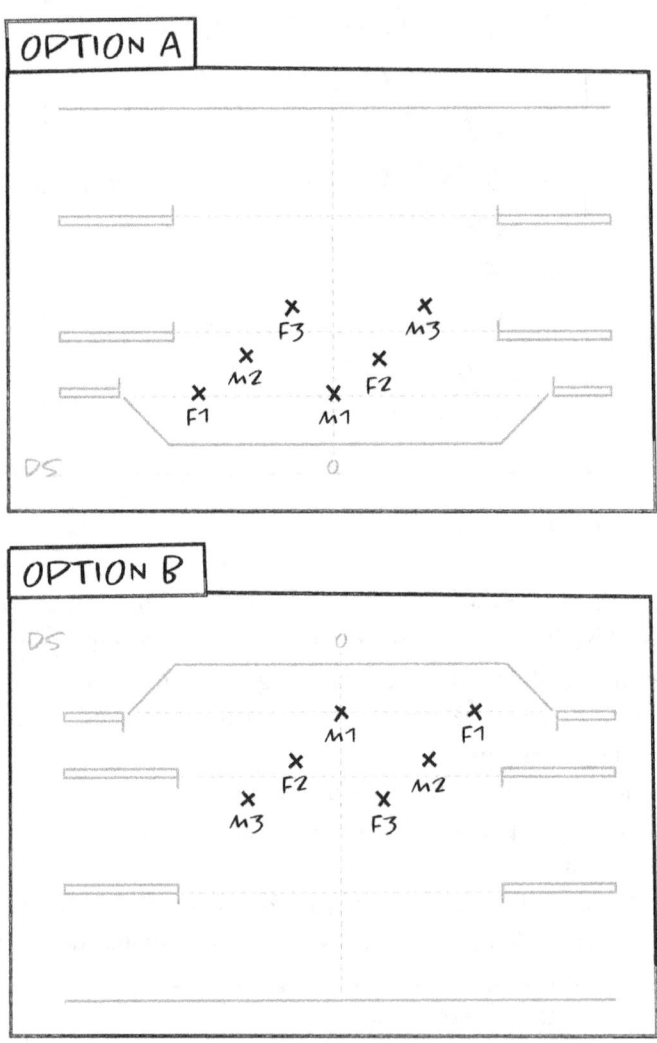

Figure 10.4 Swing map perspective

Option A shows the formation from the perspective of the audience whereas Option B shows the formation from the perspective of the performer. Your preference will probably align with the perspective from which you prefer to study video recordings of rehearsals. You will remember contemplating that choice in Chapter 9 – *Information overload*.

In the swing role, I personally preferred to chart swing maps like Option B because, using Option A, I would first need to physically turn the page upside down to work out where to stand. Next, I would sigh (and sometimes panic) because that meant having to read my coded track names upside down too! In short, maps like Option A slowed me down in practice.

> Interestingly, in my work as dance captain, I preferred to chart my swing maps from an audience's perspective (Option A) because the nature of the job requires an additional need to be familiar with the show as the audience views it.

The default of most novice swings is to chart swing maps in rehearsal from the perspective of the audience (Option A). The time and brain power it takes for a swing to re-chart rehearsal maps to suit a different preference is not to be underestimated. If you have already charted rehearsal maps like Option A but would rather have a swing bible full of maps like Option B, do not despair. Maybe, this is just an opportunity for you to acknowledge your preference so that you might begin recording swing maps from a performer's perspective next time. With any luck however, you have managed to read about this consideration before even starting your swing process. So, problem averted!

Your rehearsal blueprint can be tailored to support the perspective you prefer. Charting onto blank blueprints that resemble Option B will naturally lead you to spend more time recording variables from the back of a rehearsal room.

MINIMUM PRESENTATION CHECKLIST 2.0

To make sure swing maps scribbled in the rehearsal room make sense for as long as possible, swings satisfy the following minimum presentation checklist:

1. A title
2. A page number

3. A date
4. A DS mark
5. A centre line
6. A width descriptor

When presenting information in a swing bible, swings continue to practice some of these good habits to maximise their speed of extraction. Titles and page numbers, for example, make swing maps easy to sort chronologically which enables swings to find the map they need quickly and efficiently.

The date on swing maps, recorded during rehearsals, indicates when something was staged and will not assist speed of extraction. Instead, swings will use it to disregard out-of-date rehearsal notes when screening them. Moving forward, the assurance that your swing bible pertains to up-to-date information will eliminate any need for you to date the swing maps inside it.

Figure 10.5 Quoted E-Principle

Conscientious swings might still date their work in acknowledgement of the E-Principle that says, everything is subject to change.

It remains necessary to include a faint centre line on all swing maps because it acts as a useful tool for finding out information about tracks at a glance. Imagine, for example, the speed advantage of seeing a centre line, should any of the following rules apply:

- Stage right commence with right leg.
- Stage left face upstage.
- Stage right exit stage left.

If you manage to chart from one perspective consistently, labelling both a DS mark and a number rule (width descriptor) might seem unnecessary. While a number rule continues to be a must on all swing maps, its position on the page is flexible. You may, for example, compensate for lack of space on a swing map by drawing your number rule at the top of your map as opposed to the bottom. To account for any uncertainty about which way to hold the page up, a DS mark is the only and essential label that yield relief without fail. When time is of the essence, this small detail could make a remarkable difference to your speed of extraction.

The primary purpose of a number rule on all swing maps is to help swings accurately position themselves as well as understand their relative distance from other tracks. Sufficient spatial awareness however cannot be guaranteed unless a swing can be accurate about both the width and depth of tracks.

Sadly, most rehearsal rooms struggle to indicate how far upstage or downstage tracks are positioned because depth is not measured using the same stage number system as width. The following are commonly used to describe depth:

- Wing flats
- Flown scenery
- Set pieces
- Show floor markings
- Lighting towers

A technical drawing of the playing space is the best drawn-to-scale indicator of where depth descriptors will be. Using one is therefore highly recommended to chart swing maps in your swing bible. So, if you have not already done so, ask your dance captain, company manager, stage manager or production manager (in that order) to share a technical drawing of the stage blueprint with you.

When the time comes for swings to chart swing maps as they will appear in their swing bible then, a different set of six required labels remain. They are:

1. A title
2. A page number
3. A DS mark
4. A centre line
5. A width descriptor
6. **A depth descriptor**

> Don't pull a brain muscle, the key difference between your two minimum presentation checklists – one for the rehearsal room and one for swing bible maps – is that the second (our minimum presentation checklist 2.0) exchanges a date for a depth descriptor. That's it!

Stick with pencil

It seems nonsensical because we are taught from a young age that anything done 'in neat' should be done in pen but, pen is final, and musicals change. For example, more practical traffic will be found over time and creatives will return to productions to implement new ideas.

When transferring your rehearsal notes to your swing bible, stay stubborn, use pencil and only pencil. If you must colour code, do so sparingly but make sure you have first considered if the same information could be presented in black and white at no expense to:

1. Clarity.
2. Your speed of extraction.

USE OF SHORTHAND IN A SWING BIBLE

Swings use shorthand techniques to record variables in the rehearsal room, so that they can pack a lot of information into fewer scribbles. Speed maps, for example, depict formations in shorthand by omitting information that can be deduced later. To make these maps fit for purpose in a swing bible, swings must plug in the missing information. If a speed map is left incomplete, the inner monologue of a swing trying to extract information from it would sound a bit like this:

> *'I need to know where Dawn stands. I cannot see Dawn on my map. I know they are opposite Alex B though. Where is Alex B on my map? Alex B is in the third row in the gap between Tim and David B. Who is opposite Tim and David B? Ross and Bob. So, Dawn is in the third row in the gap between Ross and Bob'.*

Phew, you got there in the end but if you want to be a quick swing, I suggest you convert your speed maps into completed swing maps.

On the flip side, the following basics of notation you learnt in Chapter 7 can safely carry over into your swing bible with no detrimental effect to your speed of extraction, in fact they will improve it.

Coding

So long as a swing developed a consistent coding system in the rehearsal room, the processing time needed to decode 'JMS' to mean 'James' will, by now, be no time at all. Swings should therefore feel confident to use coded track names in their swing bible at no expense to their speed of extraction.

In addition, three-letter track names take up less space on the page and so continuing to use them will only make your swing maps appear clearer. **Clear maps are quick-to-inform maps.**

Now is your last chance to match your coding system to that of your dance captain and fellow swing team. At this stage, it could mean rewiring your brain to recognise a different three initials for certain tracks. Do not let that extra effort deter you, trust it will be worth it because when a swing team records in the same language, everyone is faster.

Labelling crosshairs

In the rehearsal room swings labelled coded track names in a consistent position about crosshairs to maximise the shelf-life of their rough notes. In a swing bible, the same consistent discipline maximises speed of extraction since the eye has been trained to know where to look for a specific piece of information.

If a labelling system cannot be maintained throughout an entire swing bible, swings should at least endeavour to be consistent per swing map.

Arrows

Through the practice of a consistent arrow system in the rehearsal room, swings develop an ability to decode their arrows at lightning speed. If 'arrow' were a language, swings would strive to use a level of consistency that enables them to read and write in it fluently. Very quickly then, they are able to translate an arrow to answer questions like:

- Where is my starting position?
- Who crosses downstage?
- Where is my ending position?

> There will be times when you need to make small exceptions to your crosshair labelling and arrow system. Please make them, you likely deserve the time it will save you. In fact, some information can appear clearer on a page because it exists as a lone exception. But be warned, to make exceptions everywhere is nothing short of a jumble sale, good luck finding what you need in there.

Cues and duration

Repeat practice of recording shorthand counts and lyrics in the rehearsal room will reward you with the ability to quickly understand what they mean in reverse.

We mentioned before that musical numbers are not bound to one time signature but rather it could bounce between two or more. When things get complicated, you might find it useful to note the time signature on a swing map to be doubly sure of how to count what you see recorded.

Similarly, you might be familiar with being able to count a piece of music in slow counts or fast counts. For example, consider the fifth count, if counting a 4/4 piece of music in fast 8s:

1,   2,   3,   4,   **5,**   6,   7,   8,

Now count the same section of music in slow 8s:

1   –,   2   –,   **3**   –,   4   –,

Suddenly count 5 hits at the same time as count 3. For additional clarity about the value of counts recorded, I would sometimes need to write the words 'count slow 8s' or 'count in fast 8s' in available margin space of the relevant swing map.

PENCIL & PAPER VS. COMPUTER SOFTWARE

You might be wondering why it has taken until now to contemplate the use of computer software as a swing. For one thing, computers came into our world so that we could be quicker and more accurate. Unfortunately, in the world of swinging they threaten to slow us down especially in the early rehearsal process.

Lots of intricate details, such as obscure traffic that bobs and weaves, are much faster to draw by hand than by computer. If rehearsing an original production, blocking and choreography will likely change on a daily basis too. Why lose sleep trying to make something look pretty on a computer only to throw it out the next day?

The choice between paper and computer often boils down to two factors:

1. Which is clearer?
2. Which is quicker?

If the answer to the first question is neither, pay special attention to question two. The use of computer software can be addictive, so addictive that a swing sacrifices their downtime to fuss over a map that could be drawn by hand in seconds, at no expense to clarity.

The benefits of computer drawn swing maps are that:

- Small changes to blocking or choreography rarely constitutes drawing a new swing map from scratch.
- It is more practical to use colour because it can be easily deleted or amended.
- Swing bibles that exist digitally are lighter to carry around.

Stage Write

Released in 2012, Stage Write Software is a specialist computer program which was developed to assist swings and creative teams document the staging of productions electronically. It has been used on hundreds of professional productions to great effect.

It is important to remember however that there is no computer program that can reduce the workload of swings. Swings must chart a lot of swing maps and invest a lot of time doing so. I have worked on productions where some swings chart on paper while others use computer software and I can assure you, neither got to the finish line any faster than the other.

In my current work as a director and choreographer, using software to share swing maps between people is particularly helpful. Here, helpful is the operative word because swing maps made by a third party will never maximise your speed of extraction. If they could, I should be teaching you that there is a universal way to chart swing maps but more factually, we know it to be an incredibly personal process.

The action of sharing swing maps can also deny swings the opportunity to learn more by doing. Think of all that time, unconsciously absorbing information, you would miss out on if someone simply handed you a full set of swing maps on a plate.

Whether you choose to work with computer software or by hand, it is a good idea to chart each swing map for yourself so that:

a) Your swing maps make sense to you.
b) You ensure your maximum speed of extraction.
c) You profit from knowledge gained through revisiting information in the recording process.

In the end, most swing bibles are made up of both maps drawn by hand and drawn by computer. It is all dependent on the individual swing and the nature of what needs to be charted. If you learn to swing using a pencil and paper first however, you are better equipped to enjoy both and have the option of a never-failing method to record variables when your computer device inevitably runs out of battery.

> With a little imagination, many swings manage their swing paperwork using Microsoft PowerPoint or similar. You should of course expect to encounter challenges when working with a program that is not designed for a specific purpose.

At the end of this chapter, you should be able to:

- Understand that an effective swing bible must be presented to maximise speed of extraction.
- Confidently define Screening and Swing Bible.
- Screen and order rehearsal notes to compile a chronological swing bible that pertains exclusively to variables.
- Optimise a swing bible by adhering to a revised minimum presentation checklist and consistent use of basic notation.
- List the minimum presentation checklist 2.0 for all swing maps as they appear in a swing bible.
- Compare and contrast the practicality of charting swing maps by hand versus using computer software.

11. SPEED OF EXTRACTION

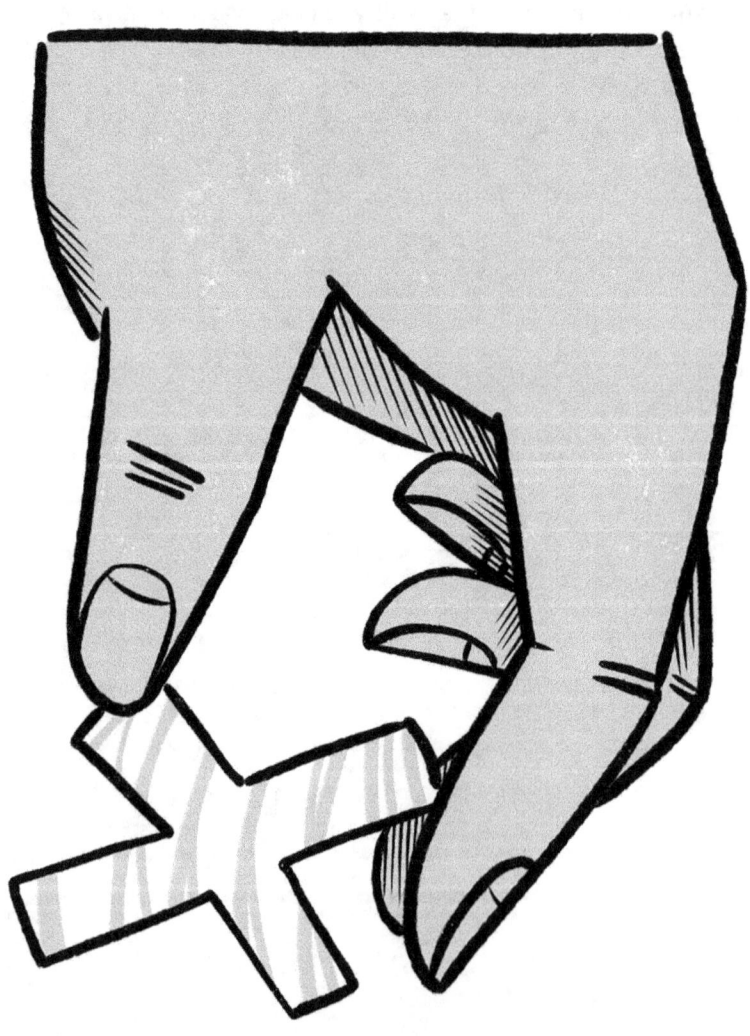

Speed of extraction
Eleven

In the previous chapter, we established some key requirements of an effective swing bible which are that one must:

1. Pertain exclusively to variables.
2. Be ordered chronologically.
3. Adhere to the minimum presentation checklist 2.0.
4. Be optimised for speed of extraction.
5. Present complete information.
6. Be available to change.

In this chapter, we will dive deeper into how a swing bible can be optimised for speed of extraction.

From taking rehearsal notes to making a swing bible, swings must switch their approach from maximising their speed of notation to maximising their speed of extraction. It is the difference between thinking 'how quickly can I write this, but do so clearly?' and 'how can I write this clearly, to read it back quickly?' In addition to contemplating swing map perspective and satisfying the minimum presentation checklist 2.0, there are plenty more ways you can present variables clearly to produce a user-friendly swing bible that makes you time-efficient when extracting information from it.

Along your decision-making way, exists an excellent opportunity to proofread your swing maps for consistent choices in coding, the meaning of arrows and positioning of labels about crosshairs. Remember the clearer you are about your basics of notation, the quicker you will be to translate it in reverse.

EXTRACTING POSITION

Often, when a track is positioned downstage (DS), their corresponding crosshair will sit close to the number rule on a swing map. As a standard, extracting downstage position is therefore quick and easy:

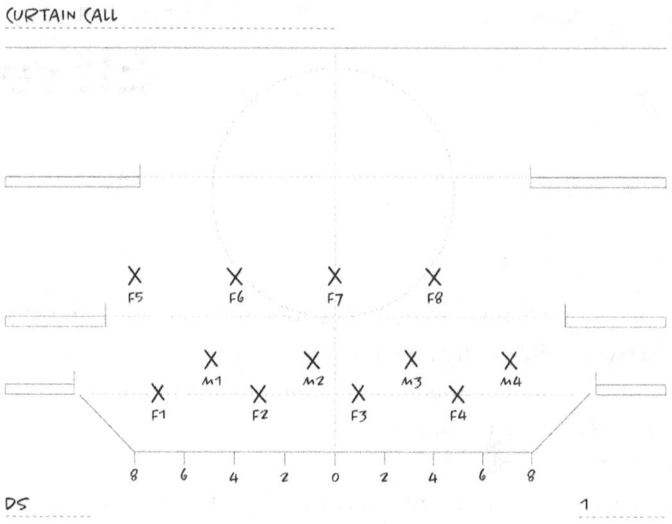

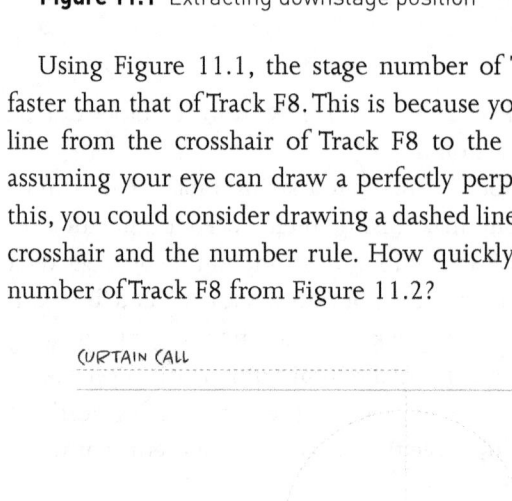

Figure 11.1 Extracting downstage position

Using Figure 11.1, the stage number of Track F3 can be extracted faster than that of Track F8. This is because your eye must draw a longer line from the crosshair of Track F8 to the number rule (and that is assuming your eye can draw a perfectly perpendicular line). To combat this, you could consider drawing a dashed line between the upstage (US) crosshair and the number rule. How quickly can you extract the stage number of Track F8 from Figure 11.2?

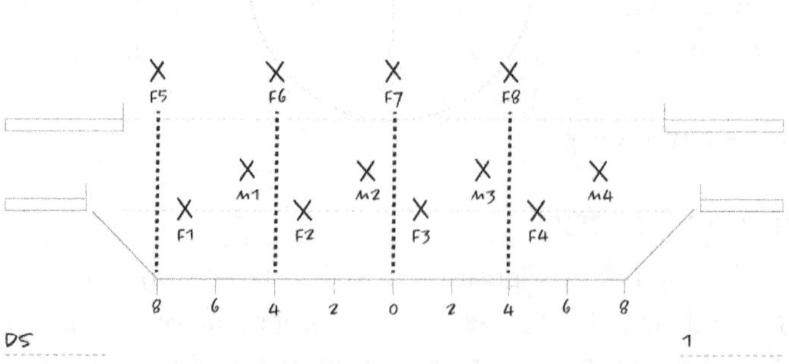

Figure 11.2 Extracting upstage position

Stage numbers are not the only layer you will want to extract from your swing maps. A few dashed lines here or there will not do any harm to your speed of extraction, but when your page starts to look like a giant game of noughts and crosses, you might want to consider using available space above, below or around each crosshair to label stage number instead, as seen in the examples below:

Figure 11.3 Labelling crosshairs with stage numbers

Where possible, it is useful to position your labels consistently so that you train yourself to know where to find specific information. Take a look at the options shown in Figure 11.3 and, not forgetting where you have consistently placed your coded track names, decide where would be best to consistently label a stage number about your crosshairs.

STORYBOARDS

In the rehearsal room, middle-charting reduces the time swings spend taking notes by reducing the number of swing maps they need to chart. Using this shorthand technique, they layer information about beginning position, traffic and ending position onto one swing map ensuring all three pieces of information can be extracted from the resultant middle map accurately. It can be so effective that rehearsal notes end up consisting almost entirely of these thrice layered maps.

To find something quickly it is better to separate information. Imagine a kitchen drawer full of knives, forks and spoons shuffled together. Everything you could want to find is in one place, but you would be quicker to find a spoon if you had separated your cutlery to begin with.

To maximise our speed of extraction from our swing bibles, we need to recover a mini storyboard from each middle map and produce three separate maps:

1. A beginning map (stationary map)
2. A middle map (moving map)
3. An end map (stationary map)

A chronological series of mini storyboards per musical number is called a master storyboard.

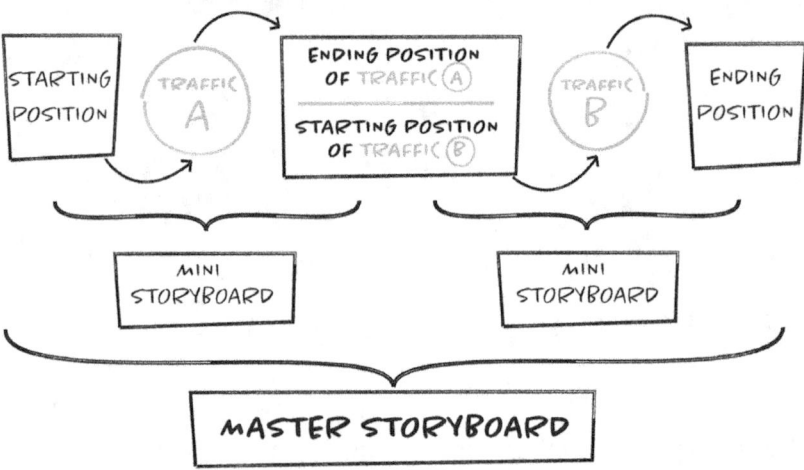

Figure 11.4 Mini & master storyboards

Each master storyboard opens with a beginning map and is closed by an end map. Inside these bookends, swing maps alternate between the moving and stationary kind because each stationary map can be viewed both as:

1. The ending position from previous traffic.
2. The starting position for upcoming traffic.

In other words, you will not literally chart three maps for every middle map you expand; most of your end maps will double as beginning maps for the traffic that follows. This is clearly demonstrated by the stationary map that sits between Traffic A and Traffic B in Figure 11.4.

> The end map of a master storyboard refers to the final stationary formation at the end of a musical number. Informally, the profession calls it 'the button'.

In general, one master storyboard will comprise of anywhere between 10 and 30 swing maps, where the upper limit represents production numbers of the juggernaut kind. Some productions are more ensemble heavy than others and the volume of your swing bible will be a direct reflection of this. In my experience, I might expect to chart between five and eight juggernaut storyboards per production, but I also swung on some of the most notoriously dance-heavy musicals.

Despite that it is time consuming, recovering mini storyboards from your middle maps will ensure that you can extract position and traffic as quickly as possible from your swing bible.

LAYERS

Layering means to show information pictorially on a map. In rehearsal notes, variables are often recorded as layers on maps out of sequence. It happens because a swing in rehearsal cares more about picking a page that has space to write on than picking a page that makes sequential sense. Equally, directors and choreographers will fast forward and rewind the rehearsal room multiple times, adding and subtracting variables until they are happy with what they see.

We know that the more orderly a swing bible is, the more user-friendly it is. So, as you layer your maps for your swing bible, remember to ask two questions:

1. Will I remember this information?
2. Is this the next variable in sequence?

The first question screens your rehearsal notes so that you do not expend time and energy presenting redundant notes. The second looks after the orderliness and consequential user-friendliness of your swing bible. Watch as I build a stationary map meant for inclusion in a swing bible with chronological layers:

Step 1: Chart position.

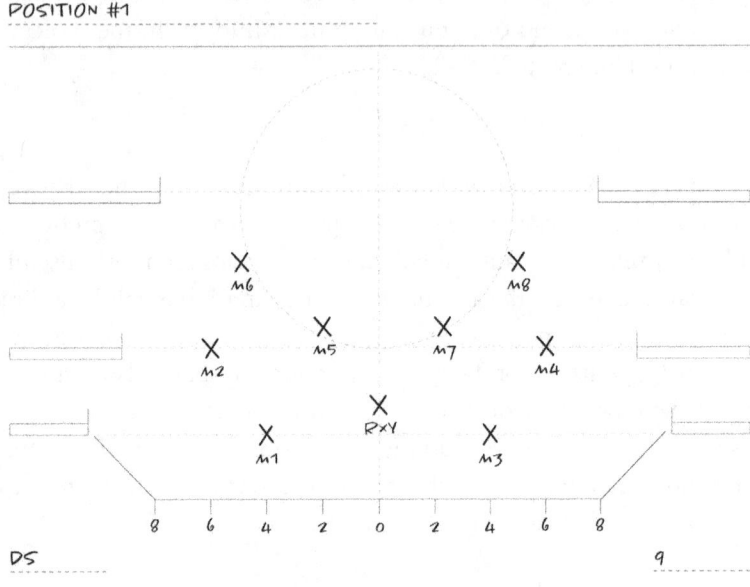

Figure 11.5 First layer: Position

Step 2: Add layer to show necessary stage numbers.

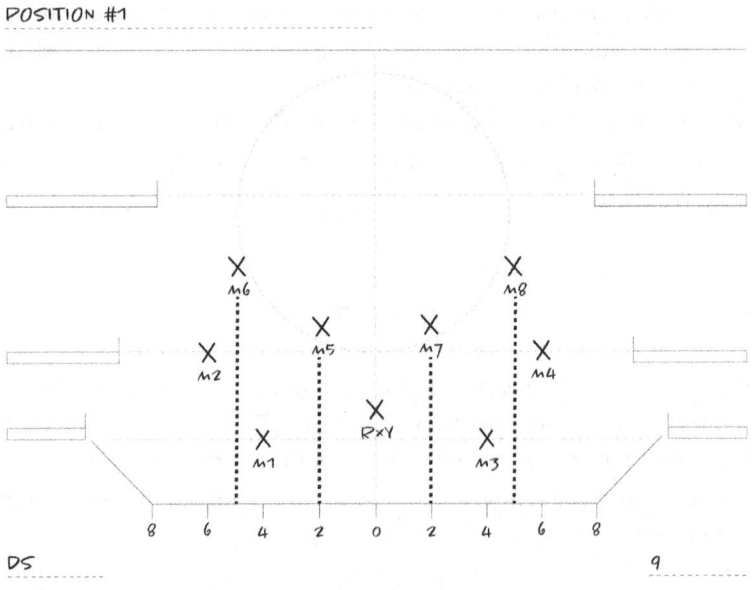

Figure 11.6 Second layer: Stage numbers

Step 3: Add layer to show which direction each track faces.

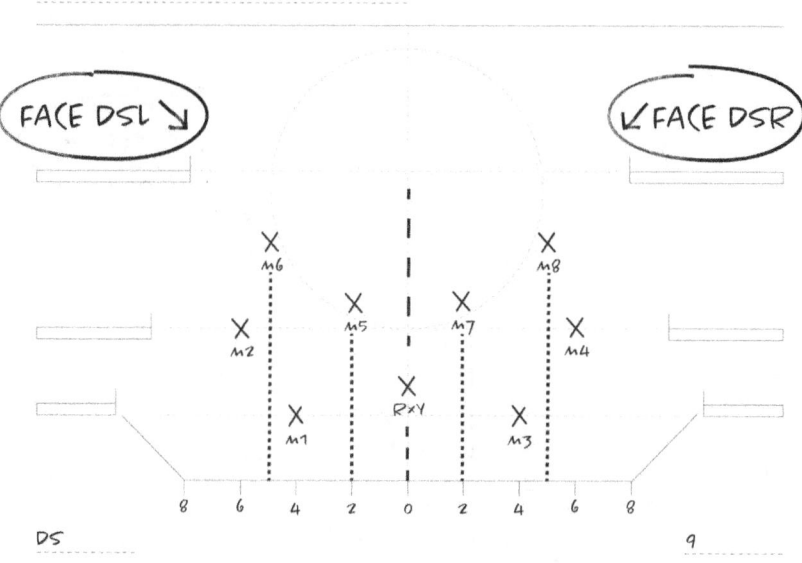

Figure 11.7 Third layer: Directional front

Step 4: Add layer to show which tracks perform a half turn and which tracks perform a full turn.

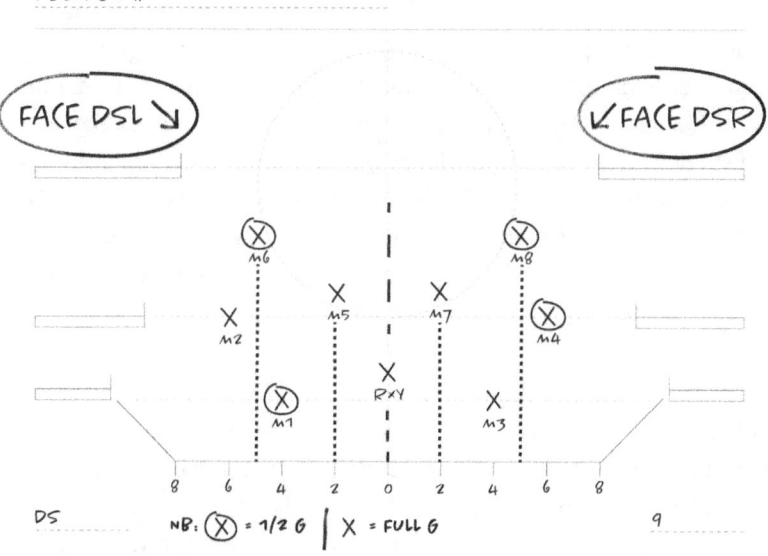

Figure 11.8 Fourth layer: Choreographic variation

Step 5: Add layer to show canon count.

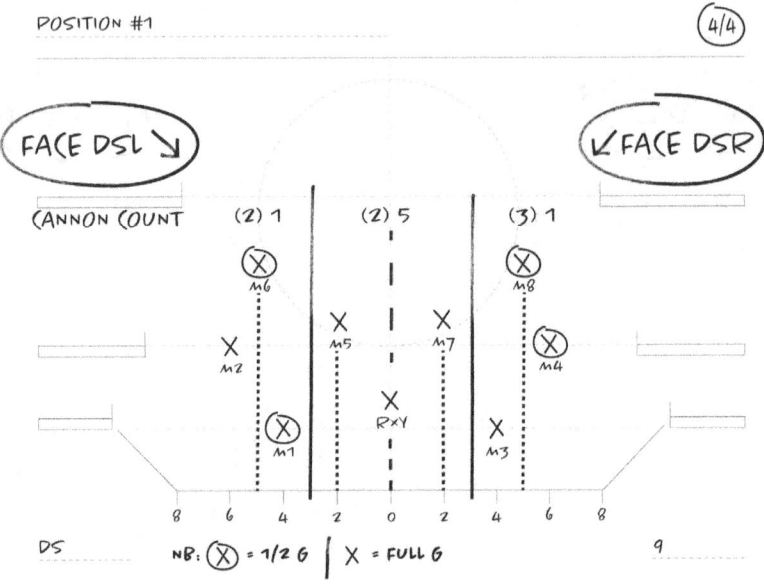

Figure 11.9 Fifth layer: Canon

Notice that step 2 (see page 146) specifies the addition of 'necessary' stage numbers. It was Chapter 8 – Speed of Notation – that we last explored the word *necessary* in the context of swinging. Then, we recorded just enough information to be able to **add** maximum detail later. Swings continue to have a vested interest in recording just enough or necessary information in their swing bible to avoid overcrowding which could decrease their speed of extraction. So, the balancing act continues, only now, swings present necessary information without impeding their ability to **extract** maximum detail, at speed, later.

Typically, swings will keep adding layers to the same map until the formation changes. Occasionally however, maps become impractically thick with layers. Imagine trying to add a sixth layer to Figure 11.9; when things get crowded, it makes it harder to extract information. Once again, **Clear maps are quick-to-inform maps.**

Swings must monitor the thickness of their layers so that they do not chart more swing maps than needed while also ensuring that none become impractically overcrowded. When layering chronologically then, swings notice when a map starts to fill up and decide to start a new one when they fear an additional layer would slow their speed of extraction.

Figure 11.10 Full map memory

I am sometimes asked, 'what's best?':

a) To finish storyboarding and then go back through your swing maps to layer variables.

or

b) To layer your swing maps with variables as you go.

The answer is a case of personal preference. Sometimes you may think you want to hammer through your storyboarding but in fact you decide to add some layers to a swing map just to break up the monotony of charting.

> The important takeaway is that, to compile the most effective swing bible, middle maps recorded in the rehearsal room must be expanded to become mini storyboards and variables should be layered in a chronological order.

SIDENOTES

There will be times when words present variables clearer than pictures. At such junctures, swings write down descriptive notes in the margin space of swing maps, hereafter 'sidenotes'. Here are some examples:

- SL passes DS of SR
- Travel for 2 × 8 starting (3)2
- Use onstage arm 1st

SIDENOTE: Information pertaining to variables written in prose.

Sometimes swings find helpful rules amid choreography or positioning that can be both quicker and clearer to write as sidenotes than present as pictorial layers. For example, in longhand, you might write:

- Tracks on an even stage number do a half turn
- Tracks on an odd stage number do a full turn

In a more ruthless, space saving shorthand you might write:

- Even = ½
- Odd = full

In fact, Figures 11.8 and 11.9 display an even shorter sidenote in the bottom margin space. The sidenote acts as a key to translate the pictorial layer which has encircled some crosshairs but not others. This is an example of how swings can combine methods of presentation – layering and sidenotes – to clearly record one variable.

The swing who charted the swing map below (Figure 11.11) noticed a rule concerning the lateral space between tracks. To increase their speed of extraction about position, they have added a sidenote in the bottom margin to describe the rule in play.

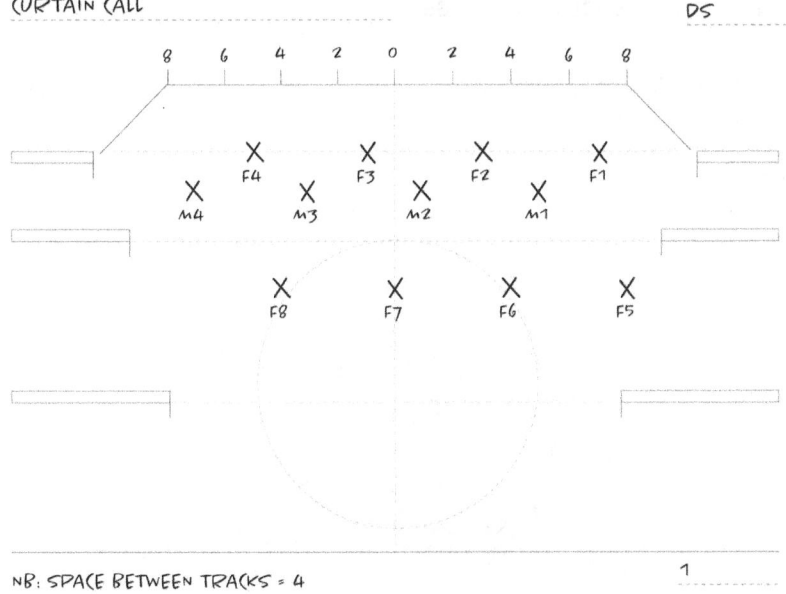

Figure 11.11 Extracting position using sidenotes

This awareness of how tracks relate to each other is an extremely valuable skill to develop. It enables swings to use their knowledge of more familiar tracks to deduce the position of less familiar tracks which, eventually, might allow them to perform independently of their swing bible.

Referring to Figure 11.11, imagine being asked to perform Track F4 after having played Track F3 in a previous performance. You might recall that F3 was positioned at 1 stage left (SL) and, using your knowledge of the positional rule, deduce that F4 must be positioned 4 spaces left of F3 at 5 SL. Such confidence to not need one's swing bible to check a variable would be described by many swings as their ultimate goal.

The skill of writing succinct sidenotes is a separate one entirely. For example, an experienced swing will recognise that 'stage right, face stage right and stage left, face stage left' can be written more simply as 'face outwards'.

> Try to recognise when the simplified instruction – face outwards – applies to all tracks because it could be classed as an ingredient and may not need recording at all.

QUICK REFERENCE GRIDS (QRGs)

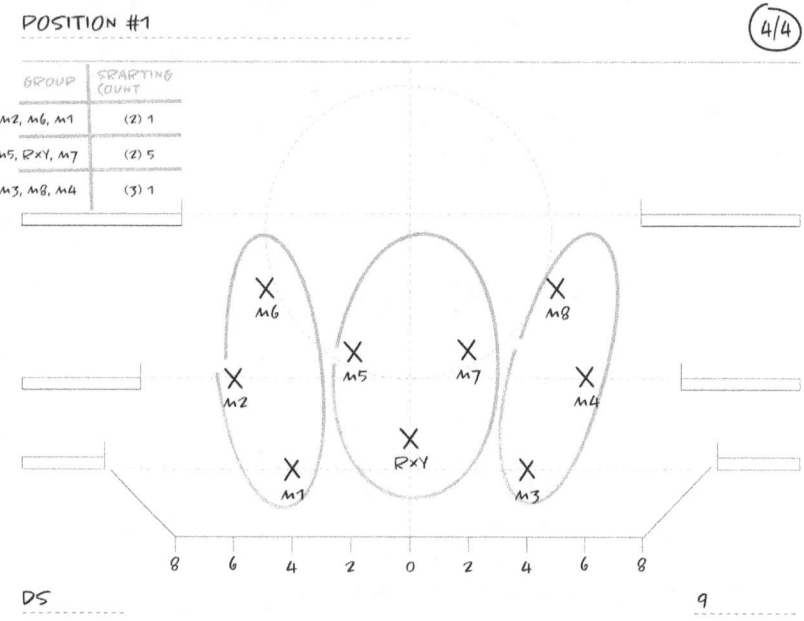

Figure 11.12 Swing map with a QRG

Variables can also be presented in tables of information which are aptly named QRGs after the purpose they serve. That is, a swing will reference a grid to quickly extract the information they need. See Figure 11.12 for an example of a QRG that stores the starting counts of tracks involved in a canon.

> QUICK REFERENCE GRID (QRG): A table of information used to speed up the extraction of a specific variable.

WHICH PRESENTATION METHOD SHOULD I USE?

The three main presentation methods, layers, sidenotes and QRGs are extremely versatile and can be used to record a variety of variables. Most commonly, they will give information about position, traffic, timing and choreographic variation. For fun advice about the most compatible presentation method for each common variable, take a look at the animated swings you see pictured. Specifically, check out which variables they bought and from where:

Figure 11.13 What swings buy at the shop of QRGs

Figure 11.14 What swings buy at the shop of layers

Figure 11.15 What swings buy at the shop of sidenotes

In the process of deciding how to present each type of variable, there are multiple factors worth considering:

First and foremost, always think about the clearest way information can be presented. For example, Figure 11.12 uses a QRG to present the same fifth layer as Figure 11.9. Which swing map makes the canon count of each track clearest to you so that you might extract the canon count of say, M5 as quickly as possible?

Secondly, you may need to weigh up the cost of choosing a less clear presentation method against the benefits of one which better supports your overall spatial awareness. Figures 11.9 and 11.12 use different methods to present the same canon in which tracks join in with the choreography at regular intervals from stage right to stage left. In this example, a QRG or sidenote could cause you to forget the relationship between formation and canon altogether. When presented as a pictorial layer however (see Figure 11.9), swings are reminded of the overall visual effect whenever they refer to the swing map. The swing that chooses a pictorial layer to present this variable would hope, in time, to know the counts of any track in this canon thanks to their knowledge of the bigger picture alone.

Thirdly, be sensitive about overcrowding your swing maps with any one method of presentation. As a swing, I found QRGs to be extremely versatile and tended to use countless of them. The trouble was, I would sometimes struggle to find the right QRG at speed because, on a page full of them, that was a bit like finding a needle in a haystack. In hindsight, to avoid too much of a good thing on one swing map, I might have thought about using a variety of presentation methods to:

a) Better preserve the clarity of it.
b) Occasionally save myself the trouble of starting a new map, just to have room for an additional QRG.

The lesson to takeaway is one I'm sure my mother, a passionate advocate of moderation, would approve of:

'Use every presentation method in moderation'

> If the safety of the performers on stage relies on a specific variable, such as moving on a specific count to be clear of a large set piece advancing, you might intentionally go against your default presentation method for a variable so that it stands out on the page as important.

You will learn through experience how you like to present certain variables and so, over time, the choice gets easier and quicker. By choosing a consistent method to present each kind of variable, you also improve your speed of extraction by training your brain to know where you are most likely to find specific information. Think about where you consistently put your keys when you get home so that you can find them again quickly.

PAGE LAYOUT

Until now, you may have only thought about drawing one map to a page, but we can also play around with our blueprint to page ratio to suit the amount of information we need a page in our swing bible to store.

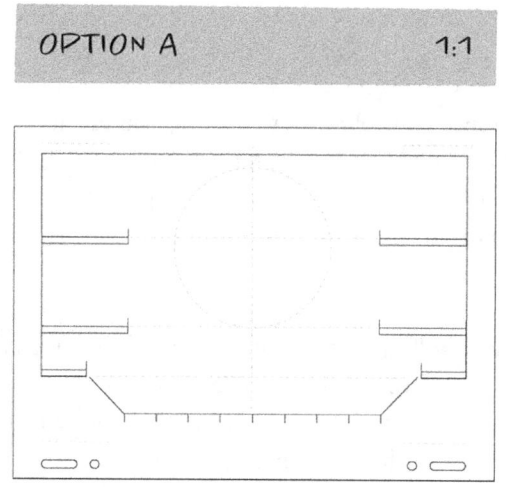

Figure 11.16 Layout A: 1:1

Option A

Table 11.1 Advantages & disadvantages of 1:1 swing map ratio

Advantages	Disadvantages
• Best for charting formation to scale.	• Increased temptation to overcrowd.
• Large capacity for multiple layers.	• Reduced margin space for sidenotes and Quick Reference Grids.

When preparing your 1:1 blueprint, it is wise to keep healthy margin space along all four edges of the page just in case you want to add the odd QRG or sidenote.

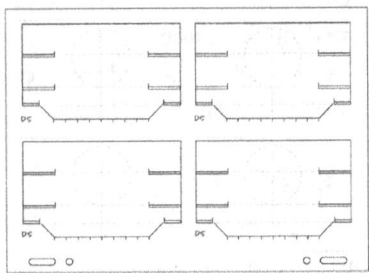

Figure 11.17 Layout B: 2:1   **Figure 11.18** Layout C: 4:1

Option B
If you scale down your blueprint by 50%, you can use the other half of your page for a QRG or more extensive sidenotes. To format your 1:2 blueprint, you might want to adjust your page orientation from landscape to portrait or vice versa.

Option C
Some sequences will move through multiple formations in a short space of time. Charting a mini storyboard on three separate 1:1 blueprints is time consuming and will make your swing bible both heavier to carry and lengthier to sift through. Instead, we can use a 4:1 page layout to chart multiple swing maps on one page and produce a sort of comic strip of quick events.

Use 4:1 blueprints wisely; the smaller the swing map, the harder it becomes to read and therefore extract accurate variables, such as position, at speed.

Option D
When you need to strike the balance between drawing multiple swing maps and preserving ample margin space for an additional sidenote or QRG, you might get playful with your page layout as seen in Figure 11.19.

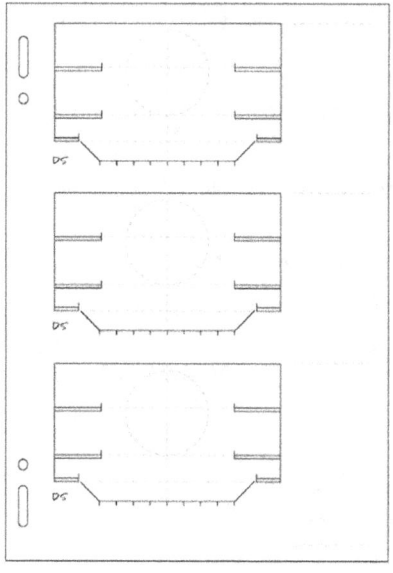

Figure 11.19 Layout D: Custom

Which page layout I found most useful changed with every production I worked on. It is a good idea to stock up on options A, B C and D at job start and replenish those most used as the rehearsal process unfolds.

CHEAT SHEETS

As an alternative presentation method to swing maps entirely, some swings construct cheat sheets. One cheat sheet will summarise the journey of a track from curtain up to curtain down. They are often written in prose or condensed into bullet points, though to liken this method to 'cheating' seems a little unfair.

Even the most prepared swings will second guess their knowledge at the last minute. At which time, it can be comforting to sneak a peek at a cheat sheet to settle any uncertainty. It is that 'sneaky' look that earns cheat sheets their name. The aspiration is of course not to need them, but swings are only human and sometimes we all need a cheat sheet.

When constructing cheat sheets, it is important to make sure they pertain exclusively to variables and are orderly by asking the same two questions as we did for presenting swing maps:

1. Will I remember this information?
2. Is this the next variable in sequence?

Per cheat sheet you might want to include information about:

- Preshow regime
- Prop collection and return
- Set handling reminders
- Entrances and exits
- Formation and stage numbers
- Choreographic variables: canon count, directional front, right- or left-lead, partner work detail
- Backstage traffic warnings
- Featured dialogue
- Reminders about safety

Unfortunately, a large part of what you would want to include in your cheat sheets won't be known until the production moves to the performance space. For example, within a preshow regime you may need to have your wig fitted at a certain time or collect your microphone from a certain place. For cheat sheets to be orderly, swings must therefore wait an entire rehearsal process before they can begin constructing them.

Figure 11.20 is an example of how you might like to format your cheat sheets:

MAXIE FORD [ENS]

SHOW LOGO HERE

ESSENTIAL TO RUN:
1. ACT 2, BIG LIFT
2. SHOE HORN FOR TRANSFORMATION W/ FRD
3. ANDREWS SISTER HARMONY

PRESHOW	
MIC:	DRESSING ROOM
1ST COSTUME:	WEDDING GUEST [//UNDERDRESS LEOTARD//]
WIG:	WIG ROOM AT 1/4
PROPS:	-
ADDITIONAL CHECKS:	MIC CHECK AT SOUND RACK AS YOU PASS

ACT 1

SC1: WEDDING RECEPTION

ENTRANCE: USC SLIDERS
SR JSH ASH MAX RYN [SL]

"SHE WORE THE SAME DRESS LAST YEAR!"

- BUSBY CAKE #1 = FACE OUT + R LEG 1ST
- BUBSY CAKE #2 = FACE IN + R LEG 1ST
- KISS THE BRIDE = OPP. HEA ON L3

(DS)
```
                X                    X
              JMS                   RYN
    X                X       X                X
   ARO             MAX      HEA              JSH
                   (3)
```
(US)

- BUTTON = STEPS W/HEA

EXIT: USC SLIDERS + STRIKE HEA CHAMPAGNE

QC SR - MILTARY SHOW GIRL   NB: CROSS VIA SUBSTAGE

---- SCENE CHANGE ----

Figure 11.20 Cheat sheet template

A cheat sheet for a specific track will leave out a lot of information about the surrounding onstage cast. When performing, I was caught off guard many times for needing to know something about another track that I had failed to include on the corresponding cheat sheet.

For the most efficient set of cheat sheets, you can manage yours much in the same way as you manage your 'I don't know' list. After having swung on for a track, revise your cheat sheet by deleting the details you did not need to check and adding anything that would have been helpful to revise.

It can be weeks or even months before you are given an opportunity to perform the same track again. After you perform a track, it can be useful to jot down what went wrong on the relevant cheat sheet to remind yourself what to look out for next time.

TRACK CARDS

Track cards are a collection of A6 notecards, or similar. They contain the same information as cheat sheets, but the information is broken up into more manageable chunks across several notecards. To maximise your speed of extraction from track cards, you could invest in different colours of notecard and allocate one colour for each musical number. That way, you can flick to an appropriate point in your track cards at speed.

The advantage of track cards is that they are more practical to keep on your person. It is certainly lighter to carry a complete set of track cards for one track to stage than your entire swing bible. You could even bind each set of track cards onto a split ring for maximum practicality.

CHEAT SHEET: A page (or more) of quick reference notes, often written in prose, which details the journey of one track from curtain up to curtain down, inclusive of any necessary backstage behaviours.

TRACK CARDS: Flashcards detailing quick reference notes, often written in prose, which describe the journey of one track from curtain up to curtain down, inclusive of any necessary backstage behaviours. A collection of track cards per track makes up one set.

At the end of this chapter, you should be able to:

❏ Maximise your speed of extracting position from a swing map.
❏ Present musical numbers as master storyboards.
❏ Confidently define Cheat Sheets, QRG, Sidenote and Track Cards.
❏ Make informed choices about how to present specific variables using a variety of layers, sidenotes, and QRGs.
❏ Vary page layout to suit the data storage requirements of each swing map.
❏ Contemplate the use of cheat sheets or track cards to present variables per track.
❏ Make a user-friendly and effective swing bible.

12. IN THE PERFORMANCE SPACE

In the performance space

Twelve

The overriding objective of the rehearsal process changes from rehearsal room to performance space; it shifts from rehearsing the actors to rehearsing the technical team. That is not to mean the actors stop rehearsing but simply that rehearsing the technical elements assumes priority. In a parallel adjustment, the priority of a swing also shifts from function to safety.

IN TECH: SWING PRIORITY

Figure 12.1 How to swing from A to B

To demonstrate this, we need to revisit an old conundrum. When a track travels from point A to point B, what is more important for a swing to learn?

A) *What* a track is doing at points A and B (the ingredients)
B) *How* and *when* a track moves from A to B (the variables)

The answer is not fixed; it depends on what stage in the rehearsal process we ask the question. In the rehearsal room, swings prioritise function meaning that they prioritise according to what information would help them to step into any track, at any given time, and sustain momentum.

DOI: 10.4324/9781003254300-13

Figure 12.2 F-Principle

Performance spaces are magical places of work, but they are also full of hazards and so, once there, the priority of swings must fall to safety.

Figure 12.3 S-Principle

Before the cast arrives at the performance space, hereafter 'the theatre', an entire team of production staff – carpenters, riggers, electricians, and engineers or "proddies" – will have loaded and fitted the set, lighting, audio and video equipment. To demonstrate the potential dangers involved, while the proddies literally build a show into a theatre, the building is temporarily classified as a construction site and must follow strict regulations until the construction phase completes.

Soon after, technical rehearsal or "tech" can begin during which a team of creatives, stage managers and technical crew choreograph some seriously hefty set pieces and machinery around moving cast. Think substantial set pieces flying from above, rising from below and moving in from the sides.

In one performance as a swing, I had to enter and position a prop toilet during scene change that happened in near total darkness. As I entered from an upstage wing and began my journey downstage, a full black cloth flew in from above and sliced me clean away from the toilet altogether. It suddenly dawned on me that I had not thought to check which wing (a variable) I was supposed to enter from and I had dangerously guessed wrong. Material fly pieces, such as blacks and cloths, are weighted at the bottom with a steel pipe called a conduit. A full black, like the one that came between me and the toilet, would have weighed somewhere in the region of 70–80 kg or the weight of a standard washing machine.

From this experience I learnt that in both tech and performance:

Choose 'being in the right place, doing the wrong thing' over 'doing the right thing but in the wrong place'.

To reiterate then, in the performance space, it is in the interest of safety that swings place more importance on knowing how and when a track moves from point A to B, which is to prioritise the variables or Option B in the conundrum.

STUDYING THE STAGE

The last run-through in the rehearsal room of a production is a guestimate in terms of where tracks need to be and when. During tech, positions are moulded around the logistics of set, wing space and auditorium sightlines and become more precise.

> It is a very different experience to watch a run through of a production along the front edge of a rehearsal room than it is to watch the same production from an auditorium. With the added benefit of distance, creatives adjust the overall look of a production during technical rehearsal. For example, they may adjust formations just to make sure the extreme right- and left-hand sides of an auditorium have a good view too.

Scene by scene the show is superimposed onto the stage with cast in full costume, wigs and wearing microphones. Meanwhile, it is standard practice for swings to observe the process from the auditorium where they will continue to record the variables, taking extra care to notice any adjustments to spacing and traffic. Now we can really appreciate why swings embrace the opportunity to practice the ingredients in the rehearsal room – it is not so easy to practice them in row F of the dress circle.

Stage numbers tend to translate well from rehearsal room to stage and so by tech, swings should have already recorded the width of tracks with reasonable accuracy. The depth of tracks however is not so easily recorded in the rehearsal room because in the absence any depth descriptors such as wings or lighting towers, it is a harder distance to gauge. As rules:

- In the rehearsal room, record accurate width and approximate depth as best you can.
- In tech, record depth as accurately as possible and fine-tune pre-existing information about width.

The number of changes that will be made during tech provide yet more reason to encourage swings to use pencil.

Depth descriptors

Upon arriving at the theatre, swings are encouraged to seek time on stage so that they can familiarise themselves with anything physical that could help them to describe depth such as:

- Wings
- Lighting towers
- Flying pieces
- Show floor panelling
- Tracks for automation

> To understand what tracks for automation are, it is best to imagine a railway track used to guide a train along its route. Some show floors also have very narrow tracks built into them which guide set pieces around the stage via a pulley or automated system.

If working from a blueprint that is a technical drawing, it is very likely that the wings will already be drawn to scale. Swings add more depth descriptors, such as lighting towers, to their blueprint based on their relative proximity to the wings.

At the very least, I strongly advise noticing something physical that aligns with the midstage line – the line that equally divides upstage and downstage – and adding this detail to any swing maps that would benefit. During tech, identifying something visual to indicate where the midstage line falls will prove invaluable when trying to assess approximate depth of tracks from a distance.

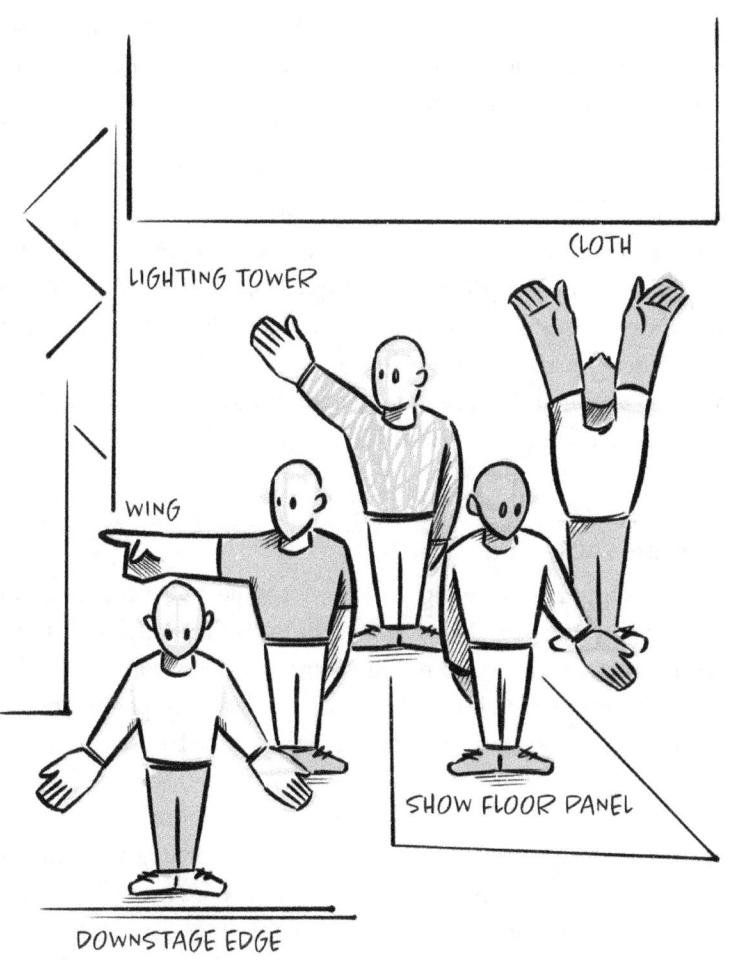

Figure 12.4 Types of depth descriptor

Width descriptors

While width is predominantly described by stage numbers on the show floor, take some time on stage to study any physical auditorium features that align with specific stage numbers such as:

- Monitors
- Fire exit signs
- Speakers

These features will help you to approximate width from afar and check your width by looking up instead of down at stage numbers in performance.

On a touring production every auditorium will be different and so the position of monitors and fire exits will change. At my most conscientious, I would take some time in each new venue to study auditorium features in relation to stage numbers.

> To avoid overcrowding, it is not necessary to depict all physical depth and width descriptors on your every swing map. A blueprint suitable for charting swing maps only labels what is absolutely necessary: the minimum presentation checklist 2.0 (see Chapter 10). Instead, mark up one blueprint with all physical descriptors, both for width and depth, and keep it at the front of your swing bible for reference when needed.

STUDYING BACKSTAGE

It is just as important for swings to learn what the audience sees as it is to learn what the audience does not see; the stuff that happens behind the scenes. Theatres are well oiled machines and so, unless you want to be the reason a production starts late or the reason a collision happens in the wings, you had best learn where each track is expected to be backstage and when.

Wig times

In the time before a performance, it is standard for wig departments to issue a schedule for cast members to have their wigs fitted. To ensure the smooth running of pre-show preparations, swings should honour the allotted wig time given to the track they are covering.

During a performance, the wig team will assist the cast to secure head pieces, apply specialist make up and affix facial hair. Swings need to pay equal attention to when these interactions happen because the timing of some may not be as flexible as others. Make sure you do not disrupt someone else's quick change or fail to complete your own because you were not seen to, by the right person, at the right time.

Prop collection

In theatre, performers are responsible for collecting and returning their personal props. Typically, novice swings will make sure they know where to collect a prop from but all too often they overlook the importance of where they return it, which, if later used by another performer, could easily result in backstage panic.

Between every performance the stage management team will reset the stage so that everything is returned to its starting position before conducting a 'shout check'. It involves, calling out an itemised list of props that are used in a production and each prop needs to be seen in the right place by the human eye before a show can begin. So, whether a prop is later used by another performer or not, it needs to be returned to a consistent place so as not to hold up show reset.

Traffic in the wings

Wings are notoriously tight spaces and any safe place to stand is fleeting. Quick changes need to be preset, set needs to be stored and, at certain times, pathways need to be kept clear for fast moving performers and crew. Until they can know confidently that they will not cause a knock-on effect to the show in motion by deviating from the norm, swings must try to mimic the exact backstage whereabouts of the track they are covering.

This includes knowing where each track changes costume, which could be side of stage or in a dressing room. There were plenty of times that I assumed my costume would be set in my dressing room only to climb four flights of stairs and find out that I should have collected it on stage level and taken it with me.

To exit one side of stage and re-enter on the other, performers need a route backstage to move between the two, known as a crossover. There may be crossover routes rear of house, via a dressing room corridor or substage, but often the quickest way to cross over is via a thoroughfare behind the most upstage piece of scenery, commonly a cyclorama or cyc.

During a performance, performers will not always be able to use an upstage crossover. Imagine the division between the stage and the upstage crossover is a pair of sliding doors, when open, any performer trying to use the upstage crossover will be in full view of the audience. On sets like this one and others, many half-dressed performers have suffered red faces trying to use an upstage crossover when they should not have.

> CROSSOVER: A route, out of audience view, to traverse between stage left and stage right.
>
> FRONT OF HOUSE: All parts of a theatre in front of the Proscenium Arch including theatre bars, foyers and the auditorium.
>
> REAR OF HOUSE: All parts of a theatre behind the Proscenium Arch including stage door, dressing rooms and the company manager office.
>
> CYCLORAMA: A backdrop, commonly a stretched piece of cloth, hung farthest upstage of all set pieces.

ENTRANCES & EXITS

In addition to learning everything there is to know about each track both on and off the stage, swings must learn how they transition between the two.

Entrances and exits may have been predicted in the rehearsal room, but nothing informs the most appropriate route to take better than being on the stage itself.

Tech provides the perfect opportunity for swings to record the entrances and exits of each track which can then be layered onto swing maps.

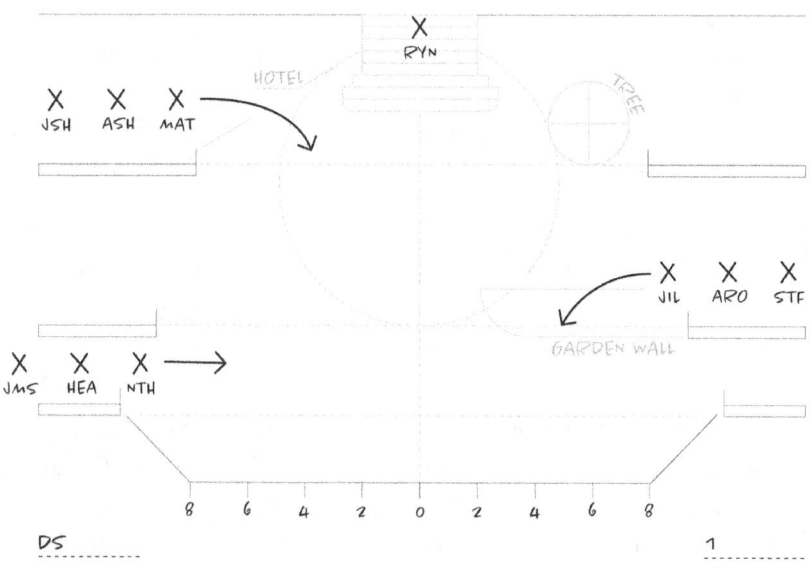

Figure 12.5 Map layered with entrances and exits

SHADOWING TRACKS

Swings may feel anxious about not being able to learn what happens backstage because they observe tech from the auditorium. A regular backstage routine is not established overnight, it takes an entire technical rehearsal, and a couple of initial performances, for onstage cast and backstage departments to work out how to move around each other in the wings. If a swing needed to step in for an absent ensemble track during tech, they would be inventing the backstage traffic on behalf of the absentee not playing catch up. There is therefore no urgency to record what each track does backstage until a show begins its performance run. This allows swings to concern themselves most with what they see happening on stage during tech.

Once a production opens to an audience, swings set about learning where to be backstage and when. We call it shadowing as swings quite literally follow an ensemble track, going wherever they go backstage during a performance. There are some ground rules about shadowing that you should know:

1. Before you shadow a track, always seek permission from the stage manager in advance.
2. To shadow, swings must be dressed in black clothing inclusive of footwear.
3. When shadowing, swings must listen and respond to backstage departments when asked to move or stand somewhere particular.

> SHADOWING: The action of following an ensemble track to learn their backstage behaviours through firsthand observation.

Despite the practice of shadowing, there will be some corners of some tracks that you may never be able to watch from a useful angle, such as a quick costume change or complex wing traffic, let us call them blind spots. If they cause you concern, talk these moments through with the relative ensemble performer or appropriate technical department. It might be even worth requesting a dry run of anything that is especially intricate at the earliest convenience of all involved.

In the early stages of a production, wings are at their busiest. Out of caution, more hands than necessary will be on deck and cast will arrive early for cues for fear of being late. To avoid overcrowding, swings may need to wait a few performances before a stage manager can permit them to shadow. Rest assured, it never takes too many performances for shows to find their rhythm and for the wings to empty.

While shadowing, you will take notes before transferring essential information to your swing bible. Commonly, swings record the backstage plots of each track on cheat sheets or track cards. The fact that swings must wait until this late stage in the rehearsal process to shadow means that, until now, they cannot begin to construct orderly cheat sheets. It is the primary reason why most swing bibles will be made up of both swing maps and cheat sheets. Understanding this to be true, the right-hand side of the SAFE Strategy – *Record the variables* – splits in two.

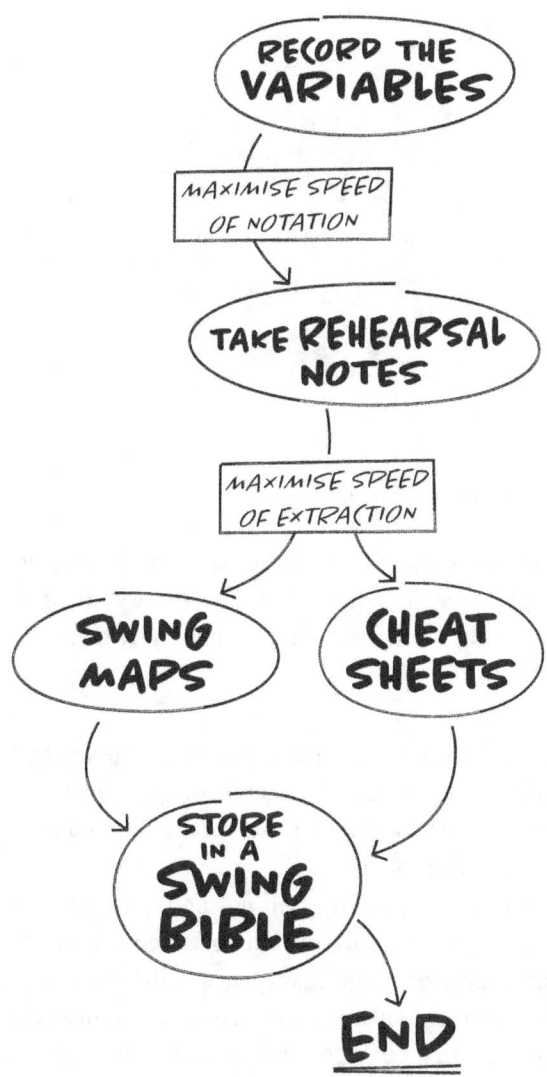

Figure 12.6 The SAFE Strategy: How to record the variables

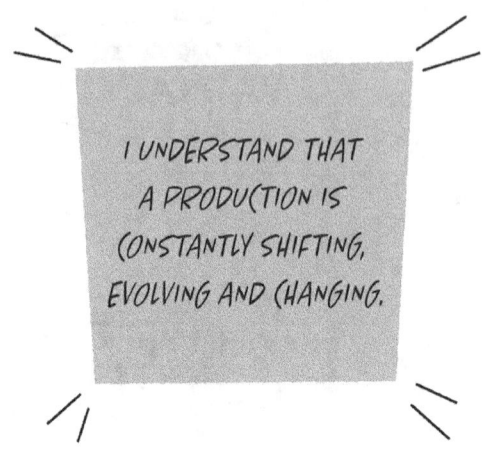

Figure 12.7 Quoted E-Principle

Once a swing has shadowed all the tracks they cover, it is still good practice to experience the wings as a shadow every now and then to stay up-to-date with any slight shifts that happen overtime.

STAMINA OF FOCUS

Since tech is notoriously slow moving, swings often spend the process gradually putting in the time that needs to go into their swing maps. They must try though to keep their eyes on the stage whenever ensemble cast are rehearsing to spot change.

From the auditorium, swings will not be within hearing distance of everything that happens. Conversations between the director, choreographer, musical director, stage manager and the onstage cast will lead to change being made but not necessarily communicated to the swing team. I found the worst conversations to miss were the private ones that happen between performers to solve minor problems. So, swings watch tech carefully and continually compare what they see on stage with the version of the production they recorded in the rehearsal room.

Of course, it is sometimes hard to tell the difference between an unheard change and human error. If you do spot something different, and you are unsure if it was intentional, it is best to add it to your 'I don't know' list and check with someone who would know better later.

Occasionally it can feel like nothing is changing and your time could be better spent charting a swing map or otherwise. Swings use their own good judgement to know when it is appropriate to work on their swing maps and when locking their eyes on the stage could be worth it for the change they see. The stamina of focus being a swing requires is precisely the reason why they have every right to feel as exhausted as the onstage cast during tech.

Figure 12.8 Swings staking out for change

Some changes will be invisible to the naked eye no matter how much of an extraordinary swing you are. You should trust that the resident creative team will make sure any critical change is relayed to the swing team in the auditorium.

REHEARSAL ROOM ATTACHMENT DISORDER

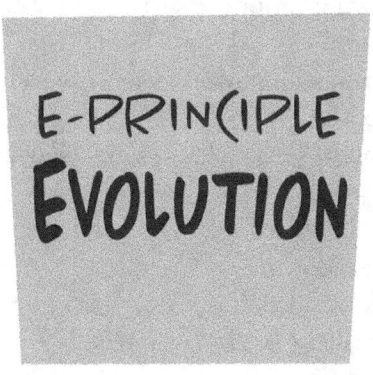

Figure 12.9 E-Principle

Swings work tirelessly during rehearsals to record as much as they can as accurately as they can in a short space of time. When they leave the rehearsal room, they hope and pray for minimal change in technical rehearsal to minimise their workload moving forward. If however, a swing becomes too attached to a rehearsal room version of a show, they can become resistant to change, resentful of it or even oblivious to it. For a more positive experience, it is much better to expect change in tech and be pleasantly surprised when it is not made.

Continuous change and the unwavering focus that the tech process demands can span multiple weeks and lead swings to burnout. Swings ward off exhaustion the same way they ward off information overload in the rehearsal room, by limiting their priorities. In the rehearsal room the first and second priorities of a swing are:

1. Serve function by learning the ingredients or variables accordingly.
2. Keep an up-to-date 'I don't know' list.

In the performance space the first and second priorities of a swing are:

1. Ensure safety by recording accurate variables.
2. Keep an up-to-date 'I don't know' list.

At the end of this chapter, you should be able to:

❑ Explain why swings prioritise variables over ingredients during technical rehearsal.
❑ Create a blueprint with physical depth and width descriptors for reference purposes.
❑ List the elements of a track's backstage activity that a swing needs to learn.
❑ Confidently define Crossover, Cyclorama, Front of House, Rear of House and Shadowing.
❑ Record entrances and exits on swing maps.
❑ Discuss the challenges swings might face to keep up with change during technical rehearsal and suggest possible coping strategies.

13. MAPS VS. CHEAT SHEETS

Swing maps vs. cheat sheets
Thirteen

When performing a specific track, you might assume it would be quicker to check a cheat sheet than search an entire collection of swing maps. By comparing the process of extraction for both, we learn that this is not necessarily the case:

Extracting information from a collection of swing maps involves navigating to a specific musical number before scanning for the track concerned.

Extracting information from a collection of cheat sheets involves navigating to a specific track before scanning for the musical number concerned.

In this context, the key to fast speed of extraction is organisation. So long as your cheat sheets and swing maps have been ordered effectively, both can be extremely quick to inform and hence most swing bibles combine a mixture of the two.

THE SAFE STRATEGY: IN FULL

The left- and right-hand branches of the SAFE Strategy we have built so far combine to reveal the strategy in full:

Figure 13.1 The SAFE Strategy

Before journeying through the teaching chapters of this book, the SAFE Strategy in its entirety (Figure 13.1) might have looked to you like a tangled web of foreign terms. Your arrival here is a promising indication that you can now reference it as a step-by-step guide to swinging in musical theatre. Let us celebrate by stepping through it together:

Step 1: Starting in the rehearsal room, swings simultaneously learn the ingredients and record the variables.

Step 2: To enable swings to get up and practice the ingredients as much as possible, swings maximise their speed of notation when recording variables.

Step 3: The products of the total rehearsal period, including technical rehearsal process, are a body that remembers the ingredients and long-life rehearsal notes that remember the variables.

Step 4: In the time that follows, swings screen, order and optimise their rehearsal notes in order to maximise their speed of extraction.

Step 5: The products of successfully screened and optimised rehearsal notes are swing maps and cheat sheets.

Step 6: Swings collate their swing maps and cheat sheets in a chronological order to make a swing bible.

Ideally, a swing has made their swing bible ahead of the first preview performance of a production. That is to say that, by the end of the technical rehearsal process, although **Step 3** describes the minimum requirement of a SAFE swing, they would always aspire to have achieved **Step 6** in the same amount of time. To manage your own expectations, the description of such an achievement as an aspiration is extremely accurate. It is quite normal for swings to still be learning ingredients and making their swing bibles alongside the initial playing weeks, and sometimes months, of the production run.

In my experience, the total rehearsal period including the technical rehearsal process can span anywhere between three and eighteen weeks. No matter how efficient you perceive your swing method to be, at the shorter end of that timescale, swings are within reason to worry about how much there is to achieve in so little time. So, not only are swings in need of a structured swing method, but they are longing for a quick one at that.

In Chapter 3 – *Strategies for every swing* – it was argued, and has since been upheld, that the most practical method of swinging is the SAFE

Strategy. Could it be possible to streamline the SAFE Strategy even further to make it not just the most practical swing method but the quickest too? To find out, swings might consider making an exclusive choice between constructing cheat sheets and charting swing maps so that they can save themselves the workload of one or the other.

CHEAT SHEETS: THE ADVANTAGES

For some the option to construct cheat sheets is a complete gamechanger and for good reason, a swing bible full of swing maps will never be able to fit into your pocket the way a cheat sheet or set of track cards can.

Space in the wings is notoriously limited and I would often struggle to find a safe nook where my entire folder of swing maps could live. If you do find somewhere, you are advised to check that the space you have found will not be needed mid show to store props, wigs, costume or otherwise with the appropriate technical departments. Conversely, cheat sheets take up much less space and some productions have even let me display mine on available wall space in each wing to support my debut or rare performance in a track.

Most temptingly, it just seems like cheat sheets would be quicker to put together than an entire collection of swing maps. Unfortunately, doing something quickly does not mean doing something thoroughly. What advantages of making swing maps would you miss out on if you weren't to make them at all?

SWING MAPS: THE ADVANTAGES

The clarity of information on your page will affect your speed of extraction and, although it is a matter of personal preference, some variables will appear clearer on swing maps than cheat sheets.

	SWING MAPS	CHEAT SHEETS
EXTRACTING POSITION	☆☆☆☆☆	☆
EXTRACTING TRAFFIC	☆☆☆☆☆	☆
EXTRACTING TIMING	☆☆☆☆☆	☆☆☆☆☆
EXTRACTING CHOREOGRAPHIC VARIATION	☆☆☆☆☆	☆☆☆☆☆

Figure 13.2 Reviewing swing maps and cheat sheets

Cheat sheets present position and traffic poorly because one cheat sheet summarises the journey of one track and leaves out a lot of information about the rest. Position and traffic are two variables that require an awareness of the bigger picture on stage and therefore swing maps are the clear winner in this respect.

Chronological cheat sheets include detail about backstage rituals which means that swings cannot begin constructing them until much later in the rehearsal process. Swing maps however can be charted as soon as the information is taught, irrelevant of any backstage business that is yet to be discovered.

In most situations, the earlier you can start something, the quicker you will finish. Here, it is more accurate to say that by starting your swing maps earlier in the production process, your total workload will be more evenly distributed over time. The ability swing maps afford swings to slowly chip away at the job ahead of them yields essential relief and plays a big part in preventing burnout.

Next, consider that swing maps work in images whereas cheat sheets work in words. When charting, layering, and annotating your swing maps, you will spend an enormous amount of time looking at an image of what the entire stage is doing at any one given time. Unconsciously, you may even start to absorb some of this information so that you can see it in your mind's eye. While you cannot take physical swing maps onto stage with you, you stand a good chance of developing mental photocopies of them, which are the next and only best thing.

To put this idea into context, imagine you are on stage but unsure where to be positioned. Your mental swing map reminds you that the overall formation is a hollow triangle. As such, you can pick out the gap in the formation and quickly jump into the right spot. This happens far more frequently than you might think, so much so that swings often joke amongst themselves about being the last to arrive in formation.

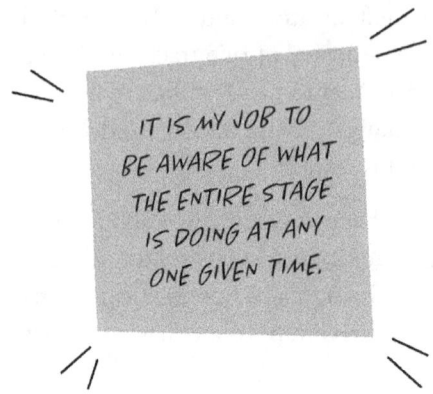

Figure 13.3 Quoted A-Principle

THE MINIMUM SWING WORKLOAD

It seems both cheat sheets and swing maps have their individual advantages which might make it difficult to have a preference about swinging exclusively from one or the other.

If you would like me to take the agony of choice away from you, we should ignore preference altogether and instead look to define the minimum swing workload. That is to know what is the minimum a swing must do to be safe and thoroughly effective.

So, as opposed to asking 'Would I **prefer** to swing exclusively from either cheat sheets or swing maps?' we should ask 'Is it **possible** to swing exclusively from either cheat sheets or swing maps?'

> If I only make cheat sheets, can I be a safe and thoroughly effective swing?

Cheat sheets and One-Track-At-A-Time swinging are similar in approach, they both treat tracks as independent entities. For the same reasons that we agree OTAAT swinging cannot produce thorough and effective swings, neither can an approach which sees the exclusive production of cheat sheets.

Let us remind ourselves of the four main reasons why OTAAT swinging, and now a cheat-sheet-only approach, fails to produce safe and thoroughly effective swings:

1. They dissatisfy the S-Principle due to inflexibility.

Figure 13.4 S-Principle

In a cut-show, a swing may be asked to split-track which is to combine one or more tracks into a hybrid one. To do this, the swing must be trusted to move from one track to another without compromising safety. Cheat-sheet-only swings are more likely to view tracks as separate entities and so their ability to split-track can come under scrutiny. When safety cannot be guaranteed, the job of the resident creative team is made harder because they must now calculate a show set-up with at least one inflexible swing that can only perform carbon copies of tracks.

2. They dissatisfy the A-Principle due to tunnel vision.

Figure 13.5 A-Principle

When tracks are viewed as standalone puzzle pieces, swings have a reduced awareness of how tracks interact with each other. They could be likened to wearing blinkers, only concerned with the view directly in front of them as opposed to surrounding them. Any reaction to sudden change of circumstance is likely be delayed as a result. For example, when a performer sustains an injury mid musical number and is unable to continue, a swing must, in the moment, think about the knock-on effect to the bigger picture and make appropriate decisions about how they could help cover the impromptu absence.

3. They dissatisfy the F-Principle due to gambling with absence.

Figure 13.6 F-Principle

As swings assemble their cheat sheets, they do so one at a time. They cannot begin this process until the production moves to the performance venue when the first performance will soon be upon them. The order of ensemble absence cannot be predicted and so, for the opening performances, it would be sheer luck if a swing had made a matching cheat sheet for the corresponding absent track.

4. They dissatisfy the E-Principle due to the inconvenience of change.

Figure 13.7 E-Principle

Upon completing their last cheat sheet, swings can forget to appreciate that productions are constantly shifting, evolving, and changing. Swings must remember that their workload is ongoing and to be a thorough swing, their swing bible needs to update as the production updates. Swings tend to avoid updating cheat sheets because it can be a more time-consuming process. For example, to update a formation, it is quicker to adjust a single swing map than it is to adjust multiple affected cheat sheets.

> If I only chart swing maps, can I be a safe and thoroughly effective swing?

In addition to meeting the level of support that cheat sheets can offer, a swing bible made up exclusively of swing maps promotes:

1. Safe swings: swing maps support any requirement to spit-track by fostering good spatial awareness.
2. Aware swings: swing maps promote a continual appreciation for the bigger picture.

3. Functional swings: swing maps do not gamble with absence because in their creation, swings always record what they can about all tracks in the playing space.
4. Evolving swings: swing maps are quick and easy to update given change.

Each of these added benefits directly combats the challenges associated with a swing bible that is made up exclusively of cheat sheets.

With all this in mind, two established facts help us to know if it is possible to swing exclusively from either cheat sheets or swing maps:

1. A swing *cannot* swing safely and effectively from cheat sheets without the support of swing maps.
2. A swing *can* swing safely and effectively from swing maps without the support of cheat sheets.

Understanding this to be true, as a minimum, all swings must do is chart their swing maps! The SAFE Strategy can be streamlined to reflect our findings and, as a result, Figure 13.8 represents a practical method for the minimum a swing must do to be safe and thoroughly effective.

The absence of cheat sheets from Figure 13.8 is indicative that they should be considered an optional tool, constructed voluntarily by swings to assist their speed of extraction.

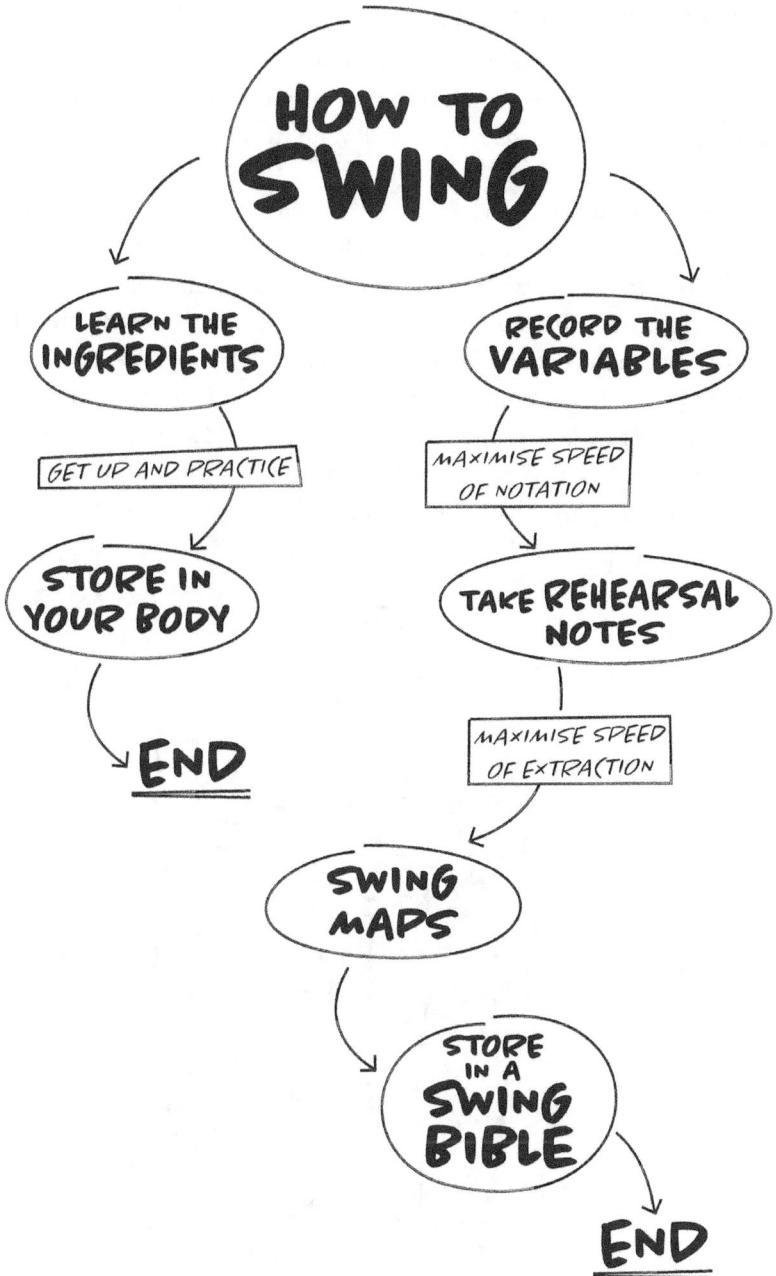

Figure 13.8 The SAFE Strategy: Fast track

HOW TO STAY IN THE FAST LANE

The workload associated with completing swing maps for every moment in a show that involves ensemble cast is not for the faint-hearted. So, it is no wonder that swings routinely deviate from the most direct path to swing bible completion.

As soon as a production has had its first dress rehearsal, the temptation to pause charting and construct cheat sheets can be overwhelming. Before you give in to temptation, remind yourself of the minimum workload to becoming a safe and thoroughly effective swing: **make a swing bible that consists exclusively of swing maps.** Any attempt you make to construct a cheat sheet ahead of this achievement can only be considered procrastination. Just as when you were a kid, you were not allowed dessert until you finished your vegetables, I advise swings not to start devising their cheat sheets until they have finished their swing maps.

Figure 13.9 Eat your swing maps

When absence requires a swing to perform in a track ahead of completing their swing bible of swing maps, they may find it necessary to pause charting and construct the relevant cheat sheet, simply to get by. To avoid getting stuck in a state of 'getting by' however, they must return to their incomplete swing maps at their earliest opportunity so that they can be described as a safe and thoroughly effective swing at the earliest opportunity too.

At the end of this chapter, you should be able to:

❏ Compare and contrast the advantages of swing maps and cheat sheets.
❏ Draw similarities between One-Track-At-A-Time swinging and swing bibles that consist exclusively of cheat sheets.
❏ Recognise swing maps as a compulsory feature of swing bibles.
❏ Recognise cheat sheets as an optional feature of swing bibles.
❏ Describe and explain the minimum workload of a swing using the SAFE Strategy.

14. SPECIALIST SWING SKILLS (S.S.S.)

Specialist Swing Skills (S.S.S.)

Fourteen

There is no doubt that by swinging once, you learn an awful lot about how you will swing again. Yet, every swing contract presents different challenges and so swings will continually encounter new firsts which will cause them to wonder 'how will I go about learning this?'

The SAFE Strategy is a base method for swinging which can be accessorised with more niche skills to suit the specific needs of a production. Think about it in terms of purchasing a car, you start with a base model before you add any desired accessories so that the car meets your everyday needs. Following a lifestyle change, the next car you buy, might warrant purchasing a different combination of accessories to meet your differing needs.

A swing that can adapt their method to fit the unique challenges of a specific production is incredibly valuable. The resultant ease they bring to the day-to-day running of theatre frequently rewards them with the reputation of being 'a good company member'.

There is some truth to the phrase 'it's not what you know, but who you know' and the part it plays in casting shows – albeit I prefer to say 'it's not what you know, but how others know you to be'. Prior to offering a job to a performer they have never worked with before; creatives nearly always seek a trustworthy reference. At this stage, the phrase 'they are a good company member' are some of the most complimentary words they can hear. Let us now explore some niche skills, outside of the SAFE Strategy as a base method, which will help you to tackle production-specific obstacles and earn points towards your 'good company member' status.

PARTNERING

When stepping in for tracks that dance, exchange dialogue or sing with another cast member, swings need to put in a little extra work to make sure they look after the consistent experience of their fellow cast when they perform.

DOI: 10.4324/9781003254300-15

No matter how confident you are, it is always a considerate gesture to approach your soon-to-be partner and ask if they would like to rehearse with you before the performance. The ideal time to ask is directly after the cast have warmed up on stage and all company notices have been announced.

Every performer is different, some will expect swings to deliver a like for like performance of the absent ensemble cast member while others will be more available to discover something new. If you feel pressured by a fellow cast member to do something differently from how you would like, try to seek a resident creative for an open and collaborative discussion about what is or what is not appropriate for the show moment in question. **Critique about artistic choices, or notes as we call them, should only come from the creative team.**

Partnering in dance works a little differently because all bodies are different and, despite your best intentions, you cannot be an exact replica of another. To make each new partnership work, grips, forces and weight placement may all have to adjust slightly.

It is always safest and more effective to rehearse partner work under controlled conditions and so ideally, swings will have experienced working with each possible dance partner at least once prior to a first performance. When the ensemble first learns the choreography, swings may be able jump in and speed date their way through each potential partnership. In any event, swings should learn partner work on the side lines of a rehearsal room with each other and grab moments to practice with ensemble cast when they can, perhaps at the start or the end of a tea break. Before you first perform in a track, you could request to run any intricate partner work in the time on stage after warm-up and company notices.

As you flit from partner to partner, you may encounter slight differences between them such that, for example, one offers you their palm turned up and another offers you their palm turned down. You could take this discrepancy to your dance captain, but rehearsal processes are an extremely busy time and so do not be surprised if having an opinion about grip, for instance, falls to the bottom of their priority list. In the meantime, mould to the method of each partner and jot down any important discrepancies as a variable. After all, given the fluctuating nature of their job, swings can be relied on to check the little things before a performance. Whereas, an ensemble cast member is probably so accustomed to doing the same thing every performance that by the time they remember to make a subtle adjustment for a swing in play, it is almost certainly too late.

> Within a swing team, it is helpful to make unanimous decisions about smaller details such as grip and learn this version as standard. That way, if two swings perform at the same time and happen to partner each other, they will know to expect a palm up or palm down and avoid any swing-on-swing panic in performance.

TRACKING PROPS

When props are heavily integrated into musical numbers and exchanged between performers multiple times, they become a virtual extension of the cast. Popular examples of this in musical theatre include the use of beer mugs in a pub setting or notepads at a press conference. By treating props as people, we can record their movements on cheat sheets and swing maps.

A cheat sheet for 'beer mug A' would look like a chronological list of the times an ensemble performer is involved in entering, passing, collecting or striking it from the playing space.

Alternatively, 'beer mug A' could be coded as 'A' and charted on your swing maps. If trying to chart props on a map that is already too busy to accommodate an additional layer, you could make a separate collection of swing maps that only exist to tell you where people and props are.

When I was a swing, I used to chart the whereabouts of props in one Quick Reference Grid per musical number and place it at the front of the corresponding master storyboard in my swing bible (see Table 14.1). I would jot down track-specific notes about where to collect or return a prop to on the relevant cheat sheet.

Table 14.1 Prop tracking

	Beer mug A		Beer mug B	
When	Collect/Pass from	Pass/Strike to	Collect/Pass from	Pass/Strike to
(4) 1	James	Ashleigh G		
(4) 5			Ryan	Ashleigh G
During dance break	Ashleigh G	Set down on bar	Ashleigh G	Stack inside Beer mug A

TRACKING SET

Sometimes, the ensemble is responsible for entering and striking pieces of set, of which tables and chairs are common examples. It is important to record the position of each piece as accurately as you would people in the interest of both safety and design.

Lighting specials are focused pools of light that intentionally highlight specific areas of stage; the resultant pool of light on the floor from a spotlight is a good example of a hard-edged lighting special. During technical rehearsal, swings should pay extra attention to the position of any moveable set pieces that are given a lighting special. It would look clumsy to position a chair out of its spotlight, but more empathetically, it could embarrass another actor if they end up in darkness when they shouldn't be.

From a distance, you probably will not notice that most show floors are covered in small colourful markings, often in the shape of a crosshair or right-angle. These are called spike marks and they mark precisely where a particular piece of set, or part of a set piece, needs to be positioned.

So that spike marks do not overwhelm a stage, if a set piece can be consistently positioned without the need to lay more, it will be. When positioned without spike marks, swings record the whereabouts of set pieces as they do tracks, using stage numbers and depth descriptors.

> SPIKE MARKS: Colour coded taped or painted marks on the show floor which indicate the precise position of performers or set pieces and ensure their consistent placement in performance.

Different set pieces will be allocated a colour of spike mark in tech. For example, blue spikes might be laid to tell a sofa apart from pink spikes that belong to a fireplace. At their earliest opportunity, when the stage is quiet, swings should find time to study the show floor to record both the colour and position of any spikes they may be required to hit.

Spike marks for chair legs can be unexpectedly problematic. Here is an example of how the position of a chair could be spiked on your show floor:

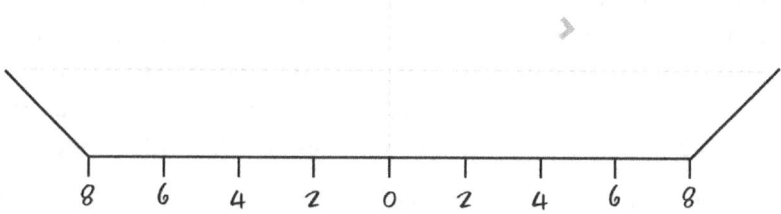

Figure 14.1 Spiking chair legs

Each right-angle helps you to know where a chair leg will be positioned, but they give no indication of the angle at which the chair will face. Which legs of the chair should be positioned inside the spike marks seen in Figure 14.1? To be thorough, make sure you are specific about what each spike mark corresponds to i.e., green spikes = stage left legs of chair facing downstage left.

> Stage managers and Assistant Stage Managers (ASMs) share a responsibility with swings to track props and record the exact positioning of set pieces. Among other reasons, they need this information to reset props before a subsequent performance and check that spike marks have not worn away over time. This is super useful for swings because if they need to check anything about prop traffic or set positioning, the stage management team make excellent people to compare notes with.

HANDLING PROPS & SET

Partnering a prop can be as intricate as partnering a person and so, again, swings seek practice in advance.

From my experience on the West End production of *Singin' in the Rain*, I know it takes a remarkable amount of practice to dance with an umbrella as effortlessly as the ensemble appear to. They, and the swings, must drill the angle of their wrist, the position of their arm and the force of their throw, all while learning how to dance against the resistance of the canopy itself.

Some other props are just plain fiddly. As part of a production, I once had to assemble, dismantle and pack away a bassoon. To learn how, I arranged time with an assistant stage manager who could talk me through each step. This is not an unusual order of events; good swings never wait for a rehearsal opportunity with props to find them but rather they find the opportunity by thinking ahead and taking initiative.

Wherever possible, try not to speculate that something will be fine. Set pieces might look light and easy to steer but are in fact the opposite and so practice must always be sought. Have you thought about set pieces that need brakes applied so that they do not move once in position? Swings may need to learn how to operate these too.

For the most part, experience with set is enough and it will not be necessary to include any instructions about handling it in your swing bible. However, as a matter of safety, I would always highlight any responsibility to apply or release brakes in my swing bible, making it especially clear on a cheat sheet.

> Please note that the stage is said to belong to the stage manager and swings will need to seek their permission if they want to practice on it. Similarly, before borrowing a prop to practice, it is polite to let a member of stage management know. When you have finished, do not forget to return it to where you found it.

SPLIT-TRACKS

A cut-show is induced when there are not enough swings to cover the total ensemble absences. They are aptly named because to make one work, dance captains and residents need to cut the equivalent of an entire ensemble track, and sometimes more, from a production. They cannot do this cleanly because ensemble tracks are never dispensable in their entirety. The nearest dispensable ensemble track you will come across is that of an onstage swing. As a result, swings are required to split-track which means bouncing from one absent track to another to cover the moments deemed most essential.

To identify what cuts to make, dance captains and residents will weigh up:

- What is easiest.
- What looks prettiest.
- What needs to happen as a matter of function.

Sometimes, to protect the look of a show, non-swings may be asked to adjust too.

On the day of a cut-show, a cover sheet will be distributed that summarises, per scene, which swing will cover which track. The cover sheet will replace or accompany the daily show set-up. This will be distributed to all technical departments and swings at the earliest opportunity. The main advantage for swings is that an advance breakdown of the cut show allows them to step through their split-track ahead of arriving at work and anticipate any tricky corners.

> Not all cut-shows are perfect and dance captains will make over-optimistic choices or forget something essential that needs covering. In my experience as a dance captain, swings would often come to me with a question or concern about their assigned split-track. Sure enough, I would revisit my cover sheet and either find a mistake or agree that a more practical choice could be made. I was always very grateful for the swings that carefully stepped through their split-track in advance because, in effect, they were natural proof-readers of my cut-shows.

In a cut-show, when a swing needs to switch tracks while on stage, that is mid musical number or scene, they may need to navigate unusual traffic. If nervous about which route to take, swings should consult a dance captain or resident director who will either advise or arrange a quick rehearsal.

The cleanest place for a swing to switch from one track to another is in the wings, they simply exit as one track and re-enter as another. In the switch however, swings may incur an additional quick change or a longer backstage journey than usual to their next entrance. To be thorough, swings must not just step through their split-track on stage but also off stage, which is to:

- Make sure they have enough time to achieve their re-entrance.
- Check where any necessary costume or wig change will happen.
- Warn relevant others of any unusual backstage traffic they will need to take.

> Cut-shows can invite high pressure and so it is easy for swings to put the needs of the show above their personal safety. The SAFE Principles help us to remember that safety comes before function and so swings must always voice concerns and never feel pressured to "give something a go" that could be dangerous.

While it is professional practice for swings to learn split-tracks by heart ahead of a performance, some split-tracks switch so frequently between tracks, and are adjusted at such short notice, that it is just not possible to do so. As a coping strategy, some learn an initial chunk and embrace the natural pauses in the show to learn the rest. Most commonly, they will focus on learning what to do in the first half of a show before using the interval to adequately prepare for the second.

SWINGING ACROSS GENDER

A swing does not need to learn *what* tracks of another gender do but, to satisfy the A-Principle, they do need to know *when* and *where* they move.

Figure 14.2 Quoted A-Principle

That said, there will be parts of tracks that are not gender specific but cannot be lost in a cut-show, such as moving set and delivering featured lines whether spoken or sung. There is a breed of swings that keep an eye out for anything essential, regardless of gender, so that they can offer a helping hand in a particularly challenging cut-show.

Also, if identified as not specific to gender, dance captains are grateful for swings who are willing to learn the choreography of tracks they are not expected to cover. In a cut-show, the knowledge and generosity of these swings might be exploited to help maintain a fuller picture and reduce the knock-on effect of show cuts on the ensemble performers – who, in general, are not as readily wired for change.

Learning material that is non-gender specific is not an expectation of swings and so it really is an example of how you might go that extra swing mile when you feel available to. The restraints of costume and wigs may mean that, despite all eagerness to help, covering tracks of another gender is just not possible. In the cases where it is, dance captains and resident directors will be readily available to impart any information that could assist a swing to perform a track they do not conventionally cover.

RECOGNISING INTENTION

To quote an old musical theatre cliché 'when it is not enough for a character to express their emotions through speech, they will sing and when it is not enough for them to sing, they will dance'.

It would be unfulfilling for a swing to execute the specifics of a track without attaching their performance to a narrative intention, not to mention unfulfilling for the audience to watch. Good swings (moreover artists) do more than just learn *what* tracks do as well as *when*, *where* and *how* they do *what*; they honour the narrative intent behind direction and choreography to enhance the story-telling of a musical.

Reassuringly, making sure to do so can reduce swing workload. So long as the swing satisfies intention, a surprising amount of direction and choreography will be up for individual interpretation. For example, where Track A waves at Track B, as opposed to learning:

1. Which hand to wave with.
2. Which count to wave on.
3. How long to wave for.

A swing covering Track A can simply learn their intention: greet Track B.

Some swings are so conditioned to learn ingredients and variables with impeccable detail that they fail to notice when they can profit from learning one intention in place of multiple ingredients and variables. It provides another incentive for swings to keep a constant check on the bigger picture in play because stepping back from the rehearsal room to cast your eye over it as a whole will make these moments easier to spot.

A swing that honours intention is often happier in the role because they are free to make artistic choices when they perform. In the above example, it is much more fun to play around with the different ways you can greet someone than mimic the ensemble performer you are covering. Equally, playful swings bring a fresh energy to the stage that is welcomed by ensemble and principal performers who may struggle from time to time with the monotony of delivering the same eight shows a week.

By contrast, if swings are made to feel that they must be clones of the tracks that they cover, it can be damaging to their sense of worth and strengthen the arguments that unfairly label swings as 'the reserve cast'.

The creative team will also stage moments which require dance and blocking to be improvised. If the onstage cast is directed to change it up performance to performance, the same will be true for swings. Of course, if you notice that two tracks routinely interact during something improvised, you might be gracious enough to learn what that is in advance.

Personally, improvisation in dance was never my strength and it will come as no surprise that I was a swing who liked to be readily prepared for all eventualities. As a solution, rather than learn the individual creations of each track, I would prepare a one-size-fits-all 'improvisation' that I could perform no matter which track I found myself covering.

BE ACCOUNTABLE

Rehearsal rooms are fast moving environments and there are several reasons why swings might not be able to observe it all.

Despite this very real obstacle, productions will not have sympathy for the swing that remarks, 'I don't know it because I have never been taught it', especially if it is heard at nail-biting short notice. Directors, choreographers, musical directors and their respective assistants are at their busiest during rehearsals and cannot be held responsible for keeping tabs on what each swing has or has not been taught.

It is the sole responsibility of swings to be fully aware of what they do not know, to learn what they can independently and to actively seek help catching up well in advance of any need to panic. Quite naturally, the practice of keeping a well-managed 'I don't know' list takes care of holding yourself accountable.

Resident creative teams do not have to babysit the learning process of a pro-active swing team and are grateful for the assurance that such swings will take an intelligent approach towards asking for clarification when they need it. As a result of this behaviour, highly valued and trusting relationships are built, which have often been known to open doors to future employment opportunities.

THE SAFER PRINCIPLES

Figure 14.3 R-Principle

Swings carry a lot of responsibility which they fulfil by working self-sufficiently. The natural consequence of spending so much time holding themselves accountable for the work that needs to be done means that they can sometimes mistake someone else's responsibility for their own.

For this reason, I like to add a fifth principle to our established set of SAFE Principles so that they become the SAFER Principles. The R-Principle can either stand for Responsibility or Remit and says that:

> I will not take on responsibility that is not mine.

I love the R-Principle because it puts an upper limit on the swing workload by empowering swings to remain within their job remit. Come the time when the R-Principle prevents you from adding something you are not responsible for to your to-do list, not only will it yield relief but you will protect your swing-worth.

REMAIN CALM

Ask any person that works in theatre 'what makes a good swing?' and an ability to keep their cool will rank high on the list of favourable attributes.

When anxiety drives me to agitation, it is generally because I am without a plan. In having access to a swing strategy, swings have a plan and are better able to feel within constant reach of calm. Specifically, the SAFE Strategy promotes composure by way of:

1. Breaking down the swing process into manageable chunks.
2. Working in harmony with the changing priority of swings.
3. Arming swings for unexpected absence.
4. Taking long-life rehearsal notes.

> 'No one will tell you what to learn or when to learn it but if it's all written down [and you can understand what you have written], your body and your brain can relax'.

5. Cultivating user-friendly and effective swing bibles.

> Of the final point made, I like to say 'Tidy swing bible, tidy mind'.

In performance, composure helps swings to be safe on stage and behave less frantically backstage, which is particularly helpful, for example, when trying to achieve a fast costume change for the first time.

Perhaps though, the specialist part of remaining calm lies in maintaining a calm exterior regardless of the nerves you feel. Nervous energy is contagious and can cause others to panic or take unusual caution. As a result, mistakes are often made which could have been avoided if panic had not been given the chance to spread.

Keeping your nerves private is easier said than done and should not be confused with hiding a lack of preparation. If you are nervous because you are unsure, it is essential that you speak up and seek the help you need but if your nerves are simply part of the thrill, consider if the show might stand a chance of running smoother if you refrain from advertising them.

> Commonly swings experience nerves because they are so keen to deliver a spotless performance. The artwork you see in this book has been drawn by my good friend and ex-swing teammate, Dan Ioannou. On my first contract as swing, he noticed my commitment to precision and hence gave me the greatest piece of advice I could have asked for, 'let go of the idea that your first performance will be perfect, it won't be'. As of that moment, I would always remember that my job as a swing was to serve function first and my own standards of performance second. A mantra that quietened my inner perfectionist and calmed my performance nerves on every swing job that followed.

SWING SELF-CARE

There is no denying that the workload of a swing is greater than that of an ensemble member, or at least in the outset. The right to adequate rest however – whether through sleeping, socialising or otherwise – is universal. Often, an increased workload causes a swing to work feverishly until exhaustion.

Satisfying the minimum presentation checklist on every swing map and keeping an 'I don't know' list are two healthy habits that contribute to swing self-care. They allow swings to take the rest they need because they can be assured that:

a) No matter how much time passes, their notes can be understood.
b) They are fully aware of their blind spots.

When I practice yoga, I am often reminded that expert yogis listen to their body and take rest whenever they need, whereas novice yogis tend to ignore stress signals to meet a premeditated expectation of themselves. The same applies when swinging, expert swings take rest when they need because in the long run, rest will help them to perform better. The stereotypical swing brain however often finds it difficult to permit rest, which is why I consider it to be a specialist skill.

Be an expert swing, rest when you need to.

At the end of this chapter, you should be able to:

❏ Recognise the value of being a good company member.
❏ Suppose how you will tackle some niche swing scenarios such as partnering, prop and set handling.
❏ Confidently define Spike Marks.
❏ Proofread split-tracks as soon as they are assigned.
❏ Comment on the expectation of swings to cover across gender.
❏ Use narrative intention to enhance your performance, reduce your workload and improve your overall swing experience.
❏ Hold yourself accountable for your own learning.
❏ Describe expert swings as calm and rested.

15. HOW TO LOOK AFTER YOUR SWING BRAIN

How to look after a swing brain

Fifteen

It does not matter your expertise, experience or field of work, we are all better at our jobs on some days than others. Physical fatigue aside, we often forget that our minds have a powerful influence on our ability to perform. Swing minds can suffer the opinions that others hold about the swing role which can affect both their happiness and quality of work. Instead of waiting to be tested by mental challenges, among which projected attitudes towards swinging are one, swings can anticipate them and ward off any knock-on feelings that could affect their job performance.

KNOW THE MYTHS

There is no question that swings are admired figures in musical theatre but there are some standard remarks which, once heard so many times, can make a swing feel more pitied than admired. It can be both tiresome and difficult to remain positive when surrounded by flippant comments that insist you are hard-done-by. Some of my personal bugbears included:

> 'I could never do what you do'
> 'It's sad that swings aren't better recognised for what they do'
> 'In America swings are cast first and paid better'

The last speculation irritated me so much that I flew to New York to speak directly with the swings in the business and separate fact from fiction. I could not be sure the British were not just attached to the idea that the grass has to be greener elsewhere. I did find that the pay packet for swings was healthier across the pond, but it was also healthier across the full spectrum of performing roles in musical theatre. Proportionally, swings are no more recognised monetarily in North America than they are in the UK.

As for the order in which performers are cast, the individual requirements of productions vary so much that there simply cannot be a hard and fast rule. Given that swings cover the full skillset of the ensemble however, I would suggest most casting teams find it illogical to cast their swings before their ensemble.

MANAGE BLAME

It is not uncommon for mishaps in a performance to be traced back to something a swing did. If they were not directly involved in an incident, it could be that their previous traffic was a catalyst for the incident in question. This will be true some of the time but since swings are a constant variable, it is very easy for onstage cast members to unfairly shift blame onto swings. The important thing for any swing to remember is that blame wastes time where solution could be sought. If you find yourself in a situation where the finger is being pointed at you, rightly or wrongly, ask one question 'what can I do to help next time?'

REMEMBER YOUR 'WHY'

Stereotypically, performers take pride in their job by meeting their own standards of performance but swings feed their pride by:

1. Enabling a musical to function smoothly.
2. Helping other performers to meet their own standards of performance.

It is such an important program shift that this book tried to kickstart it as early as Chapter 2 – *What is a Swing?* – and since then, the F-Principle has served as a constant reminder that function matters more than the satisfaction of a swing's performance ego. With function at the steering wheel, swings can dismiss any inner critic that might suppose, 'you could have sung this or danced that better' which, overtime, could harm their confidence.

Applause plays a big part in helping someone to be proud of themselves, just imagine the first time a baby does anything, adults clap. Unfortunately for swings, their list of firsts is so extensive that the applause inevitably dies out and much faster than you might think. As soon as a swing makes their performance debut, their every future performance, whether in a new track or not, fades into the everyday.

It is not uncommon for a swing debut to be entirely upstaged by a higher profile one such as, an understudy going on for the title character. In this scenario support forces such as directors, choreographers, musical directors and dance captains will more likely devote their attention to the understudy. Swings meanwhile will be expected to be self-sufficient and they may not be shown due appreciation after.

When I was a swing, if I felt a lack of thanks or congratulations, I tried to remember that the applause at the end of every performance is recognition enough. It represents that without swings, musicals would not be possible, something I took immense pride in.

A JACK-OF-ALL-TRADES BUT MASTER OF NONE

When swinging using the SAFE Strategy, swings gain from having an awareness of the bigger picture. Unfortunately having an awareness of the whole (all tracks) hardly ever feels as satisfying as knowing something smaller (one track) incredibly well. This is the often-frustrating fate of SAFE swings.

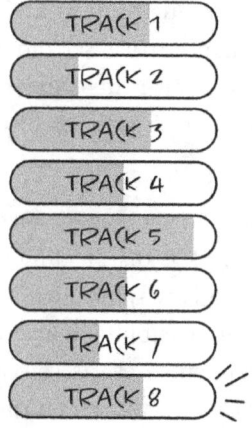

Figure 15.1 The SAFE Strategy progress bar

When they are subsequently required to step into a track in rehearsal, SAFE swings must be accepting of the inevitable mistakes they will make. Rehearsal processes tend to last anywhere between four and twelve weeks. For swings, it is a long time to feel like they are not performing to the best of their ability and so they must fight the temptation to change tact and start perfecting one track at a time. Trust in the full process, by keeping your eyes on the bigger picture for the long haul, the all-encompassing knowledge that you crave will arrive in time.

ALWAYS PRESENT, SKILLFULLY UNSEEN

In the rehearsal room, swings endeavour to get up and practice the ingredients as much as possible. They must however accommodate the needs of the creative team before their own which means to be careful about where they practice so as not to pull focus from the rehearsal in progress. As a result, they face a tricky conundrum; they must find a spot from which they can see and practice everything being taught without being seen practicing.

Similarly, when a musical director needs to hear the full ensemble sound without the support of swing voices, swings may be asked to be 'present but not heard' too.

> Once a production has officially opened, swings will be used to assist the rehearsals of understudies by informing the space as ensemble bodies. It is a fantastic opportunity for swings to make up for lost practice time during tech and better acquaint themselves with the performance space, set and props. Yet again though, they must attempt to embrace this time all the while accommodating the needs of the understudies before their own.

It is not totally ridiculous to say then, that a good swing is very good at being invisible. The drawback is that, feeling invisible traditionally takes its toll on self-worth which is why, in the context of swinging, I preach the importance of viewing invisibility as a seriously impressive skill.

One of the best compliments I ever received when I was a swing was post show from the musical director who turned to me and said, 'I didn't even notice you were on'. Arguably a musical director in the orchestra pit has the most intimate view of a production. Not only that, but they watch the show night after night and so have a sensitive radar for the slightest detail that differs from the norm. If they were not aware that I had performed, that had to indicate that I had done my job particularly well.

To be clear, the compliment I took away was not that I was unremarkable on stage but that I did not disrupt the experience of the audience or those who perform regularly. Other than making sure that a show was able to tell its story from start to finish unhitched, maintaining the routine experience of the onstage cast was always my secondary aim. On a good day, I might even satisfy my third objective, which was to be proud of my personal performance.

THE PERFORMER BUCKET LIST

There are certain events associated with working in musical theatre that most performers hope to experience. They include media shots, press night performances, live concerts, award ceremonies, television appearances and soundtrack recordings. Unfortunately, to ensure their availability to cover absence at short notice, swings are not guaranteed to participate. When a production first opens however, multiple glamourous opportunities happen in quick succession and having to sit them out one after the other can sting a little.

Most productions do their best to include the swings where they can. For example, on the most recent production of *Young Frankenstein* in the West End, formations were adjusted to incorporate the offstage swings so that they too appeared in the production shots alongside onstage cast, which consequently appeared on the front of the Garrick Theatre for all of London to see.

When they cannot take part in certain events, swings are better to accept it as a sacrifice they make for the thrill of getting to be a swing day-to-day.

THE SWING SENTENCE

You will meet some industry professionals that believe every performer should swing once. Their reasoning stems from the idea that you can only truly appreciate the work of a swing by experiencing it for yourself. Of course, this is not the only way to cultivate appreciation, we can also achieve it through effective education which makes sure every performer knows what it takes to be a swing and how to work alongside them in a mutually supportive way.

The same people, and a few more, might tell you that once you have been a swing, you will pigeonhole yourself as a swing for future work. If that were true, the advice that 'every performer should swing once' almost certainly would not exist.

I would argue that your career path rests much more heavily on being able to discuss your honest hopes and dreams with your agent than it does on the one swing contract you accept. More factually, I know plenty of performers that disprove the pigeonhole theory by gathering CVs that are full of both swing and ensemble credits. Jeremy Jordan, Karen Olivo, Jonathan Groff and Jerry Mitchell all made their debuts as a swing before becoming the household Broadway names we know today.

In the swing role, your continual development will be hotly maintained. If willing, the number of skills you stand to add to your skillset to cover that of an entire ensemble is endless. Peers of mine have learnt how to play musical instruments, speak new languages and even, fire breathe.

Without doubt, swings are some of the most talented performers we have on our stages and so you can rest assured that the only swing curse you will suffer is the luxury of choosing where your embellished skillset will take you next.

SWINGS IN THE PUBLIC EYE

The internet is heaving with articles that intend to elevate public appreciation for swings. Typically, the headlines will read something like *Swings Are The Unsung Heroes Of Theatre* and *Swing: The Hardest Job In Musical Theatre*. Problematically, I believe these headlines only remind readers that swings can be overlooked and miss the opportunity to incite change through positive education. If the latter were happening, similar articles would not appear on my social media newsfeeds anywhere near as regularly as they do.

Why Did I Choose to Be a Swing? is an article I wrote and published with an intentionally positive title to help disassociate the swing role from historical underappreciation. I encourage you to do the same, engage in positive conversations about the swing role and you will not only upgrade your swing experience but the experience of all swings as we slowly teach others about the joys of swinging.

At the end of this chapter, you should be able to:

❏ Dispel some common swing myths.
❏ Take pride in a primary responsibility to serve show function.
❏ Maximise your swing potential by protecting your swing self-worth.
❏ Be a positive advocate for swings.

Outro

When I was offered my first swing job, I scoured the internet and libraries for a text that could teach me exactly what a swing does but I always came up upsettingly short. I wanted guidance that offered more detail than a vague instruction to *cover the ensemble*. I needed an insight into the impending scale of the job in hand and to be inspired by the tactics of my swing predecessors.

Unitl now, the total absence of a swing method has caused the swing workload to gain a reputation for being immeasurably big. The type of performers who attract the swing role therefore lean towards the happy-work-trojan kind who, with great urgency, are deserving of an easier ride. More despairingly, I know too many performers who would be brilliant swings but have shut a door on the experience because what they imagine the job to be feels too daunting.

Figure 16.1 The SAFE Strategy

To make the role more manageable for all and accessible to a wider pool of performers, the question 'How do you swing in musical theatre?' needs to be answered, shared and taught.

The most direct route to becoming a thoroughly effective swing is by following the SAFE Strategy to completion (see Figure 16.1). Nevertheless, I would forgive you for saying that the full process still looks like an alarming amount of work. In Chapter 13 – *Swing Maps vs. cheat Sheets* – we counted a total of six steps to be exact but what if I told you we could reduce that number of steps to just two? They are:

1. Learn and remember *what* every track does.
2. Have access to *when*, *where*, and *how* tracks do *what* in the form of swing maps.

Once stripped of excessive detail, the minimum workload to swing effectively does not look so bad at all:

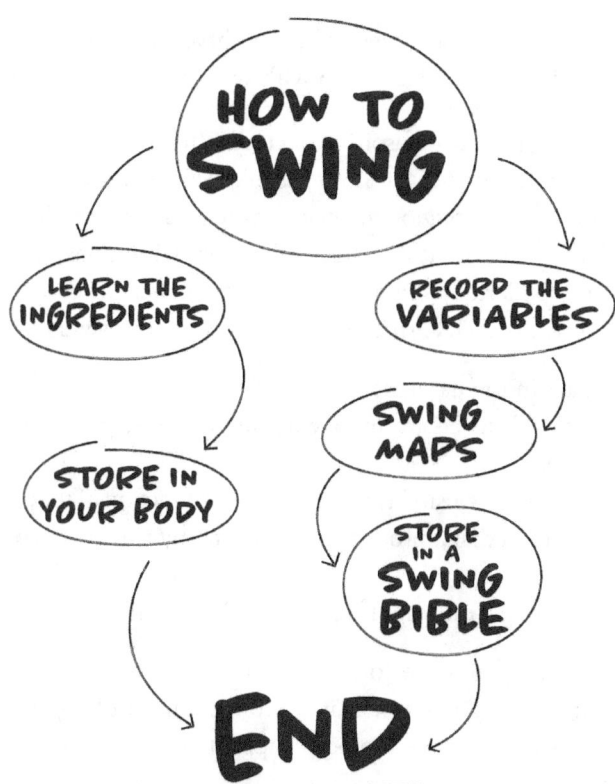

Figure 16.2 The SAFE Strategy: Simplified

For a long time, I have been told the skill of swinging cannot be taught because it is too dependent on the individual. But when I realised how many swings share in the same two-fold process as me, I could not pass up the opportunity to share it as a jumping-off point.

It will take discipline to make your swing process as pure as the one seen in Figure 16.2. I promise you, the monotony of charting maps and the temptation to write cheat sheets too soon will come knocking. If I am honest, I gave into it every single time during my decade as a swing, but I was always comforted to know there was an end in sight and it was defined by the completion of my swing maps.

In exchange for the initial hard work swinging demands, you will love seeing theatre through a completely different lens and meeting endless exciting opportunities to grow, learn and develop as a performer. I may be biased, but there is no other job quite as satisfying and I wish for every performer to know it.

Now it is time for you to harness what you have learnt and discover how you can apply it to your relationship with swinging in musical theatre.

If you are a swing performer, aspiring or current, remember to reference this book as your swing advisor and not your ruler. Whether your most valuable takeaway from our exploration together is as hefty as learning how to make a swing bible or as trivial as numbering the pages within one, as you swing in your own wonderfully unique way, I hope you take care of yourself by quietly keeping the SAFER Principles in the back of your swing brain:

S – I will act in the name of safety first.

A – It is my job to be aware of what the entire stage is doing at any one given time.

F – My primary responsibility is to facilitate the function of the production.

E – I understand that a production is constantly shifting, evolving and changing.

R – I will not take on responsibility that is not mine.

If you are a non-swing performer, I trust that you have information enough to know confidently why it is a role not meant for your path and that you feel better equipped to both support and be supported by your future swing colleagues.

To whoever you are reading this, swing, non-swing or friend of a swing, thank you for picking up this book and I wish you to enjoy spreading the message with me, far and wide, 'swings and ensemble performers are siblings; different in skill but identical in value'.

Glossary

APRON: An extension of the stage floor which projects into the auditorium of a Proscenium Arch stage.

ALTERNATE: A performer who regularly plays a principal role but has less scheduled performances across the production run than the performer cast in the role concerned. They are often cast when a role is physically or vocally demanding.

AUTOMATION: Motor operated scenery.

BLOCKING: General term given to the movement of tracks on stage not classified as choreography.

BLUEPRINT: A floorplan of the stage, or playing space, including performer access routes, drawn to scale from a bird's eye view.

CANON: When the same ingredients are performed at staggered times causing a ripple effect.

CAST: The entire collection of performers that could potentially play in a production.

CENTRE LINE: Imaginary line through the playing space lengthwise which divides its total width in half.

CENTRE STAGE: The centre of the total playing space calculated as the point of intersection between the centre line and midstage.

CHARTING (MAPPING): The technique of plotting the width and depth of tracks as co-ordinates on a bird's eye floorplan of the playing space to produce swing maps.

CHEAT SHEET: A page (or more) of quick reference notes, often written in prose, which detail the journey of one track from curtain up to curtain down, inclusive of any necessary backstage behaviours.

CODING: The process of abbreviating track names to enable fast notation.

COMPANY MANAGER: Central administrative role responsible for overseeing the day-to-day running of a theatrical production. Primary duties include handling payroll, scheduling, press, events, holidays, health and safety, ticket requests, training and bridging communications across all departments.

CROSSOVER: A route, out of audience view, to traverse between stage left and stage right.

CUE: A time indicator which informs precisely when to take action.

CUT-SHOW: Term given to a reduced version of a production that has been reconfigured to meet the demands of extreme absence or technical hindrance.

CYCLORAMA: A backdrop, commonly a stretched piece of cloth, hung farthest upstage of all set pieces.

DANCE CAPTAIN: A responsibility given to a member of cast to maintain the choreographic quality of a production. Duties include leading daily warm-up, facilitating understudy rehearsals and informing show set-ups.

DIRECTION/DIRECTIONAL FRONT: An instruction to describe the angle something is facing or a track calls their 'front'.

DOWNSTAGE: General term given to the area at the front of the playing space or that which is nearest the audience.

DRESS REHEARSAL: A run-through of the production in the performance space with all technical and design elements in play. The first dress rehearsal sits between the end of technical rehearsal and the first performance.

FRONT OF HOUSE: All parts of a theatre in front of the Proscenium Arch including theatre bars, foyers and the auditorium.

INGREDIENTS: Information, recalled from memory, pertaining to what tracks do; what steps they dance and what words they say.

LAYER: Pictorial representation of a variable on a stationary map.

MARK-UP: An outline, often taped, of the set dimensions on the rehearsal room floor.

MIDDLE CHARTING: To solely chart the moving map of a journey to increase speed of notation.

MIDSTAGE: Imaginary line across the playing space which divides its total depth in half.

MASTER STORYBOARD: Chronological collection of swing maps describing the whereabouts of all tracks for the duration of one musical number.

MINI STORYBOARD: Chronological collection of three swing maps – beginning, middle and end – which describe the three stages of any single journey taken by a track or tracks.

ONSTAGE SWING: A cover for absent ensemble tracks who also possesses their own ensemble track.

OFFSTAGE SWING: A cover for absent ensemble tracks who does not possess their own ensemble track.

PIT STOP: A brief pause taken by a track along the course of a longer journey.

PLAYING SPACE: Traditionally refers to a stage but denotes the areas used by performers to deliver a performance in view of the intended audience.

PORTAL: Soft or hard dividers used to divide wing space into separate wings such that one portal may act as both the downstage boundary of an upstage wing and the upstage boundary of a downstage wing.

PROSCENIUM ARCH: A stage whereby all but one length of its perimeter neighbours a backstage area. The remaining length neighbours the audience. Sometimes referred to as an 'end on' stage, the audience looks onto the stage through a frame, or 'archway', to view the action, or 'scene', behind.

PRODUCTION MANAGER: Overseer of technical elements of a show co-ordinating with producers, designers and show crew to ensure productions are set up safely, on time and within budget.

QUICK REFERENCE GRID (QRG): A table of information used to speed up the extraction of a specific variable.

REAR OF HOUSE: All parts of a theatre behind the Proscenium Arch including stage door, dressing rooms and the company manager office.

RESIDENT CREATIVE TEAM: In-house directors, musical directors and choreographers that attend the day-to-day running of the show to maintain show quality on behalf of the creative team: directors, musical supervisors and choreographers.

REVOLVE: An embedded turntable in the show floor which, when operated by automation to spin about a central point, moves people and/or set.

SCREENING: The process of filtering rehearsal notes to disregard ingredients and transfer variables only to a swing bible.

SHADOWING: The action of following an ensemble track to learn their backstage behaviours through firsthand observation.

SHOW SET-UP: Daily summary of absence and break down of cast covering.

SHOW WATCH: To observe a performance from the auditorium. Commonly, undertaken by cast to enhance professional performance and creatives to monitor show quality.

SIDENOTE: Information pertaining to variables written in prose.

SPEED CHARTING: The art of recording enough information about where tracks are positioned so that comprehensive and accurate swing maps can later be derived.

STAGE LEFT: Term given to the area of playing space that is left of centre when facing downstage.

SPIKE MARKS: Colour-coded taped or painted marks on the show floor which indicate the precise position of performers or set pieces and ensure their consistent placement in performance.

SPLIT-TRACK: A hybrid ensemble track performed by swings when required to cover more than one ensemble track in a single performance.

STAGE MANAGER: Overseer of the onstage and immediate backstage areas, responsible for their safe and smooth day-to-day running. Crucially they lead the technical rehearsal process as the primary communication channel between the director, technical departments and cast.

STAGE NUMBERS: A graduated measure of stage width used to accurately position performers and maintain formation over time. Commonly marked discreetly along the downstage edge of the show floor. Zero equates to centre and numbers ascend moving outward.

STAGE RIGHT: Term given to the area of playing space that is right of centre when facing downstage.

STANDBY: An offstage performer who is available to play a principal role under unscheduled circumstances such as in an emergency. They are cast for roles that are physically or vocally demanding or have time consuming makeup, wig or wardrobe requirements.

SWING BIBLE: The collective term given to documentation used by swings to assist the retention of information that cannot be recalled from memory.

SWING MAP: A pictorial representation of the state of play on stage, from a bird's eye view, notably demonstrating the whereabouts of tracks and set pieces.

SWING: A cover for ensemble tracks.

TECHNICAL REHEARSAL: The process of rehearsing a production into the performance space from a design perspective. Technical departments such as costume, wigs, stage management, sound, lighting and automation will rehearse and learn their show around what has been created in the rehearsal room.

TEMPLATE TRACK: Conceived ensemble track used by swings to embody a standard combination of ingredients against which all ensemble tracks can be closely compared.

TRACK: The complete journey of one onstage cast member in a performance, inclusive of their backstage activity.

TRACK CARDS: Flashcards detailing quick reference notes, often written in prose, which describe the journey of one track from curtain up to curtain down inclusive of any necessary backstage behaviours. A collection of track cards per track makes up one set.

TRAFFIC: A variable describing the pathway a track takes between two stationary positions.

UNDERSTUDY: A responsibility given to a member of cast to cover a principal or supporting role in case of absence.

UPSTAGE: General term given to the area at the back of the playing space or that which is farthest from the audience.

VARIABLES: Recorded instructions that can change and affect the ingredients, differentiating one track from another. Variables predominantly inform the answers to *where*, *when* and *how* tracks do *what*.

WING: An access pathway used by cast to enter and exit the stage or playing space.

About the author and illustrator

Contributors

ABOUT THE AUTHOR

Jaye Elster began her career as a professional actress and quickly found her feet in both dance captain and swing roles. West End credits include *Half a Sixpence* (Noël Coward Theatre), *Matilda the Musical* (Cambridge Theatre) and *Singin' in the Rain* (Palace Theatre) – a production she later returned to as associate choreographer and continues to look after internationally as additional choreographer. Today, she works predominantly in creative roles, traversing directorial and choreographic collaborations. Outside of performing, Jaye is a passionate guest lecturer for some of the UK's top musical theatre institutions. She would say her early reputation as a swing is largely responsible for her continued success in an ever-challenging industry hence her fervent pursuit of better swing training and support for future young performers.

ABOUT THE ILLUSTRATOR

Dan Ioannou worked professionally as an actor for several years working on productions spanning theatre, tv and film playing both featured ensemble and swing. Credits include *Matilda the Musical* (Cambridge Theatre), *Singin' in the Rain* (Palace Theatre), *Billy Elliot* (Victoria Palace) and *Beauty and the Beast* (2017 Film). Today, Dan works primarily as a multi-disciplinary graphic designer where he harnesses his experiences in the performing arts to better influence his understanding of visual languages.

Index

Note: **Bold** page numbers refer to tables and *Italic* page numbers refer to figures.

accountability 202–203
accuracy: of position 63–64, 74, 102, 166, 196; of video recording 115
acting with others 194
after stage left *see* Law of Traffic, The
allocation, cover 25
alternates 10
annotation 183; arrows 80; crosshairs 74–77, 135; layering 103–104, 106, 142–143, 145–152; layout 155–157; minimum presentation checklist 131–134; Quick Reference Grids 152; sidenotes 86; *see also individual entries*
appropriate mindset 14–15, 17, 21–23, 207–212
apps *see* software
arrows 77–80, 78–80, **80**, 95–96, 102–104, *104*
artistry 22, 194, 201–202
attitude 193, 208–212
audition routine 31–32
automation 116, 166
Awareness Principle (A-Principle) 19–20, *19*, 36; cheat sheets 183; dissatisfaction of 185, *185*; gender specific tracks 200, *200*; speed of notation 99–100, *100*; swing maps 183

backstage tracks 168–174
basic shapes *vs.* crosshairs 74
behavioural code of conduct 17, 22–23, 203
blame management 208
blocking (scene work) 85–86, 201–202
blueprint 43–45, *44*, 65, 131, 155–157, 168

broken arrow 80, **80**
busy scenarios 66–67, 74, 82–84, 102, 111–122, *121*

canon (build-up) 105–107, **105**, *106*, 148, 154
career management 4, 14, 211
cast 17; definition of 8; offstage 8–10; onstage 8–9
cast change 35–36; minimal 53–54
character traits, page 202–204, 213
charting (mapping) 44, 65, 72–77, *73*, 96–97, *97*, 99, 100, 106, 117, 128, 130–135, *130*, 137–138, 142, 143–150, *151*, 152, 155–156, 166–168, 182–183, 187–191; middle 101–102, *101*; speed 96–98
cheat sheets 157–160, *159*, 179–191; advantages of 182, *182*
choreographic rule 103, 133, 147, 150
clarity 69, 91, 94, 134, 136, 137, 154, 182, *182*; in relation to consistency, page 64, 71, 104, 107–108, 134–136, 141; in relation to cramming/overcrowding 42, 44, 82, 84, 86, 98, 129–130, 149, 155–156, 168
coding/track abbreviation 69–72, *71*, 135
coloured pens/pencils/highlighters 41–42, 75–76, 134, 137
company: family tree 7, 12, *12*, *13*; manager 9, 10, 18; mid-contract, joining 36–37; structure 7–13
consistency 64, 71, 104, 107–108, 134–136, 141; of shorthand 107–108
continuous arrow 80, **80**

225 Index

Index

costume 4, 35, 50, 166, 170, 172, 199
counts: shorthand for 86–89, 89, 105, 136, 148
covering system 2, 3, 28, 98
creating 'time' 46, 61, 126–127, 166, 194
crosshairs 74–76, 74, 75, 104, 135, 143
crossover 169–170
cues 84–89, **91, 105**, 106, 107, 136, 148
cut-show 28, 185, 198–201
cyclorama 170

dance captain 13, 18, 61, 131, 198, 199, 201
depth descriptors 72, 166–167, 167
direction (directional front) 102–105, 103, 104, 147
dress rehearsal 116
duration: shorthand for 89–91, **90, 91**

ensemble 2, 7, 8, 12, 50, 216; mindset 13–14, 17; specific advice 45, 82, 115, 116–117, 119, 202
entrances 43, 44, 44, 165, 170–171, 171
equipment 40, 41–43, 45, 160; cheat sheets 157–158, 159; swing bible 29
etiquette (general and situational) 10, 22, 199, 202–203, 208
Evolution Principle (E-Principle) 21–22, 21, 41; colour 75, 76; minimum presentation checklist 2.0 132; OTAAT Strategy 27, 27, 187–188, 187; rehearsal room attachment disorder 175–176, 175; shadowing 174; video recording 116
exits 43, 44, 44, 170–171, 171
expectations 194; management of 45, 120–122, 181
extracting: variables 141–160; position 141–143, 142, 143, 151, 153

fast lane, stay in 190–191, 190
favours 101, 201
flexibility: backstage behaviour 169
flowchart for runaway rehearsal rooms 121

FOMI (Fear Of Missing Information) 111–112
formation 19, 20, 45, 52–53, 62–66, **76**, 77, 99, 130, 131, 133–134; button 145; charting 72–75, 99, 130, 146; speed charting 96–97; in tech 165
front of house 170
full map memory 149
Function Principle (F-Principle) 20–21, 20, 46; dissatisfaction of 186, 186; performance space 163–164, 164; priority 66–67, 67, 112–113, 112; satisfaction of 121–122, 121, 122

good company member 193

half counts 89
harmonies 49, 54–55
How to Swing in Musical Theatre 37; book objectives 4–5, 14, 33–37, 42; method 30–32, 30, 56, 56, 93, 126, 173, 180–182, 180, 189, 214, 215, 215

'I don't know' list 45–47, 102, 174, 176, 202, 205
independent traffic 78–79
information overload 102, 111–122, 176, 205
ingredients 30–32, 49–51; SAFE Strategy for 56, 56
intention, recognizing 201–202
intersectant traffic 79–81, 84

job performance, measure of 208–209

labelling crosshairs 74–75, 75, 104, 135, 143
Law of Traffic, The 78–82; after stage left 81–82
layering (layers) 77, 146–148, 153, 170, 195; for extraction 142–143, 145–152; rehearsal notes 84, 102, 103, 105–106
learning by studying 36, 117, 138, 183

lighting 50, 72, 116, 133, 164, 166–167, 167, 196
long-life notetaking 60–66, 62, 63, 69, 71, 74, 77, 125, 204; centre line, drawing 63; date or time, adding 61; downstage, marking 62; stage width 63; title 61
lots (of counts) 87–88
lyrics: shorthand for 107

maps (charts) *see* charting (mapping)
mark-up 43
melodies 40, 54–55
mid-contract hires 36–37, 53–54, 98
middle charting 101–102, 101
midstage line 167
minimum presentation checklist 71, 205; in rehearsal notes 64–65, 65, 85, 97; in a swing bible (minimum presentation checklist 2.0) 131–134, 141
minimum swing workload 184–190, 215–216
moving maps (middle) 76, 77, 78–81, 84, 102, 144, 171
muscle memory 50, 51, 54, 55, 66, 76, 127
myths, knowing 4, 207–208, 211

nerves 50, 204
notation 68–91; speed of 92–108
notebook 42, 47, 61, 66
notecards (track cards) 43, 160, 172, 182
number rule *see* stage numbers

offstage cast 8–10
offstage swing 8–10, 13
One-Track-At-A-Time (OTAAT) Strategy 25–29, 26, 27, 52, 184; appropriate use of 52, 120; *vs.* cheat sheets 184–188; *vs.* SAFE Strategy, The 32–33
onstage cast 8–10
onstage swing 8, 9, 13, 34–35
organisation: of cheat sheets 160; quality of being 46, 113, 132, 202
OTAAT *see* One-Track-At-A-Time (OTAAT) Strategy

page layout 146–148; 155–157, **155**; cheat sheets 159
partnering 193–195, 202
pas de deux (partner work) 158, 194
pattern 20, 22, 54, 97, 99, 100, 183
pencil 41, 75, 134, 137–138, 166; case 41–42
perfectionism 21, 204, 209
performance space, in the 116, 163–176, 196, 210
performer: types of 7–10, 14–15; bucket list 211
permissions 114–115, 172, 198
perspective, map 130–131
pit stops 83–84, 83, 84
position 19, 53, 63–64, 133–134, 146, 150–151, 165; charting 72–76; extraction of 141–143, 142, 143, 151, 153; speed charting 96–98
pre-production 38–47, 86
presentation methods 145–155, 153; cheat sheets 159
pre-show regime 10, 47, 158, 194, 199
priority: in rehearsal 66–67, 112–113; in performance space 163–165; second 113
production manager 39
production numbers 85–86, 145
production run 21, 181; mid 36, 53
professional practice 4, 22, 115, 118, 119, 193, 203, 208–211; code of conduct 17
props: collection of 169; handling 197–198; tracking 195, **195**
publicity events 211

QRGs *see* Quick Reference Grids (QRGs)
quarter counts 88–89
Quick Reference Grids (QRGs) 152, 152, 153, 154, 195

reaction speed 19, 50, 186
rear of house 169–170
recording variables 59; basic techniques 59–66, 69–91, 107; canon 105–107; directional front 102–105; increased speed of 93–102

redundant notes 126–128, 145
rehearsal process 2, 21, 35–36, 53, 60, 93, 116, 137, 157; in performance space 163, 172 181, 183, 194, 209
rehearsal room: abbreviations 94–96; attachment disorder 175–176; priority 66–67
remain calm 203–204
Remit Principle (R-Principle) *see* Responsibility Principle (R-Principle)
resident creative team 18
Responsibility Principle (R-Principle) 203, 203
rest 60, 64, 71, 75, 98, 128, 137, 205
revival 35–36, 61
ring binder 42
role responsibilities 1, 3, 8, 17, 34, 169, 198, 199, 202, 203, 203, 210; allocation 25; vocal harmonies 54–55
ruler 42

SAFE Principles, The 17–23, 18–21, 23, 216
SAFE Strategy, The 30–32, 30, 31, 37, 125, 126, 193, 214; in full 180–182; for learning the ingredients 56, 56; minimum swing workload 184–189, 189, 215; progress bar 30–31, 209, 209; for recording variables 173; for studio rehearsal 93
SAFER Principles, The 203, 203, 216
Safety Principle (S-Principle) 18, 18, 47; dissatisfaction of 185, 185; key considerations 100, 100, 155, 198; performance space 164
scatter graph 73
scene work (blocking) 85–86
score 39–40; musical structure 87, 136
screening 127–128, 127, 145, 181
script 39–40, 85–86
self-care 21, 60, 120, 121, 205, 207–212; *see also* rest
self-sufficiency 46, 50, 113, 172, 194, 196, 198, 199, 202–203
set: handling 197–198; tracking 196–197, 197

shadowing 171–174,
Shoes the Musical 1, 4
shorthand: consistency of 107–108; for counts 86–89, 89; for duration 89–91, **90**, **91**; increased speed 93–97, 101–107; formation 69–76; for lyrics 107; SAFE 86–91, 89, **90**, **91**; in a swing bible 134–136; traffic 76–84
show set-up 4, 10, 13, 199
show watch 9
sidenotes 86, 147–148, 150–151, 151, 153, 154
Singin' in the Rain 4, 197
software (apps) 137–138
SOLT Agreement for West End Theatre Artists 3
Specialist Swing Skills (S.S.S.) 193–205; accountability 202–203; gender specific tracks 200–201; intention, recognizing 201–202; partnering 193–195; props, tracking 195, **195**; props and set, handling 197–198; remain calm 203–204; self-care 205; split-tracks 198–200; tracking set 196–197, 197
speed: charting 96–98; of extraction 141–160; map 96; of notation 93–108
spike marks 196–197
split-tracks 28, 185, 198–200; and onstage swings 9, 35
S.S.S. *see* Specialist Swing Skills (S.S.S.)
stage: management 116, 117, 118, 164–165, 169, 197, 198; numbers (number rule) 63–66, 63, 65, 72, 96, 97–98, 133–134, 142–143, 142, 143, 146; studying 165–168; types of 62
stamina of focus 22, 174–175, 176, 190
standbys 10
stationary maps (beginning and end) 72–75, 101, 103, 144–145
step-by-step method 33, 180–181, 180, 215; layering 146–148; OTTAT Strategy 25–26; variables, extraction of 179; variables, recording of 60
storyboards 143–145, 149–150, 156; master 144; mini 144

swing 1–15; across gender 98–101, 200–201; definition of 8, 12, 13; ensemble vs. 13–14; mindset 14–15, 17–23, 208; offstage 8–10, 13; onstage 8, 9, 13, 34–35; priority 66–67, 112–113, 163–165; rehearsal process 33–37; rucksack 39–43, 40; seasoned 34, 107–108; self-esteem 8, 12, 119, 202, 207–212; *see also individual entries*
swing bible 29–30, 45, 125–138, 141; content 29, 128, 172; optimising 128–130; ordering 128, 132, 145–149; ready-made 35–36; tidying 126–128, 127
swing map 44, 45, 62, 65, 72–74, 73, 86, 96–97, 99, 103, 106, 117, 128, 130, 151, 152, 154, 167, 174, 215, 216; advantages of 182–183, 182; vs. cheat sheets 179–191; digital 137–138; page layout 155–157, 155–157; in a swing bible 130–136, 141–149

target setting 181
teamwork 52, 61, 72, 114, 118–120, 135, 195
technical rehearsal 116, 163–166, 171, 174–176, 196
template track 32–33, 50–51, 56
time: management 19, 117, 136, 137, 184–189; long-life notetaking 60, 64; OTAAT swings 25–26; SAFE swings 31; signature 87, 136
timing 153; canon **105**, 106, 148, 154, 158; counts 86–89, 89; duration 89–91, **90, 91**, 136
touring productions 11, 168
track 3, 8; allocation 52, 75, 98–101; cards 43, 160, 172, 182; function machine 31; multiple, at a junction 80–81, 81; journey/pathway of 77–84, **78**; multiple, at multiple junctions 82–84; position of 69–74; props 195, **195**; set 196–197
traffic 59, 76–78, **76**, 101–102; direction vs. 102–105, 103, 104; law of 78–79, 81–82; mass 82–84; types of 78–79; in wings 169–170
tunnel vision 27–28, 27; cheat sheets 185
types of swing 8–10

understudy 1–3, 11, 119, 210
up-to-date knowledge 61, 115–117, 188; cheat sheets 160; Evolution Principle (E-Principle) 21; I don't know list 45, 113; screening 132; shadowing 174

variables 30–32, 52–53; choreographic variation 31, 106; position 72–76; presentation of 153; recording 59–67, 59; timing 86–89; *see also individual entries*
vicious circle of missing information 111
video recording 113–118; accuracy of 115; device 43; permission in rehearsal rooms 114–115; total workload 117–118, 118; up-to-date 115–117
vocabulary list 94
vocal harmonies 54–55

whole counts 88–89
Why Did I Choose to Be a Swing? 212
width descriptors: alternative 72, 168; *see also* stage numbers
wigs (facial hair) 168–169
wings (bays) 133, 165, 169–172; shorthand for 95
workload: minimum swing 184–191, 189, 215, 215; reduced 19–20; video recording 117–118, 118